Tattoo Designs Book for Men

Meaning and Symbolism in Tattoo Art

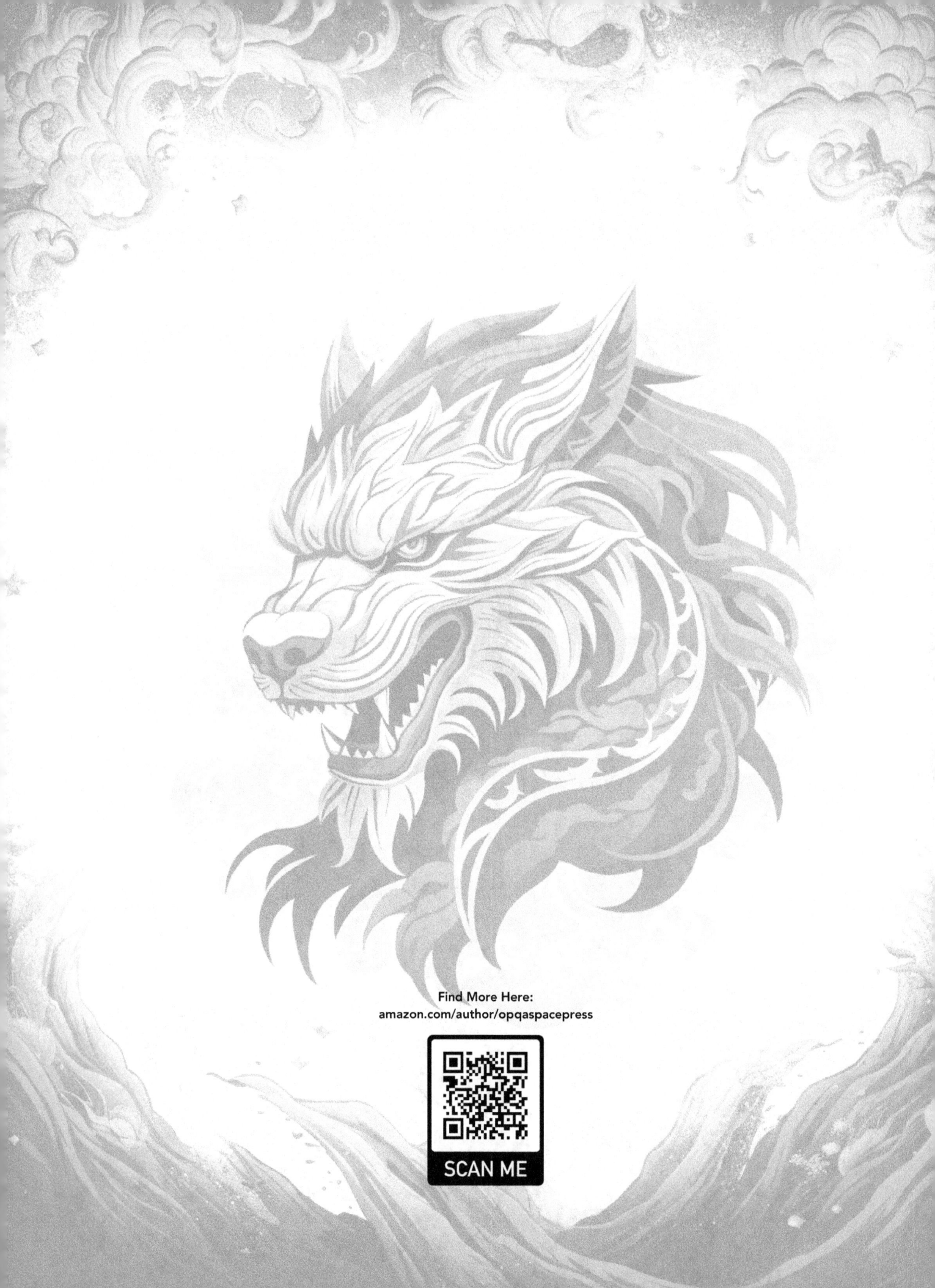

Find More Here:
amazon.com/author/opqaspacepress

SCAN ME

Tattoo Designs Book for Men

Meaning and Symbolism in Tattoo Art

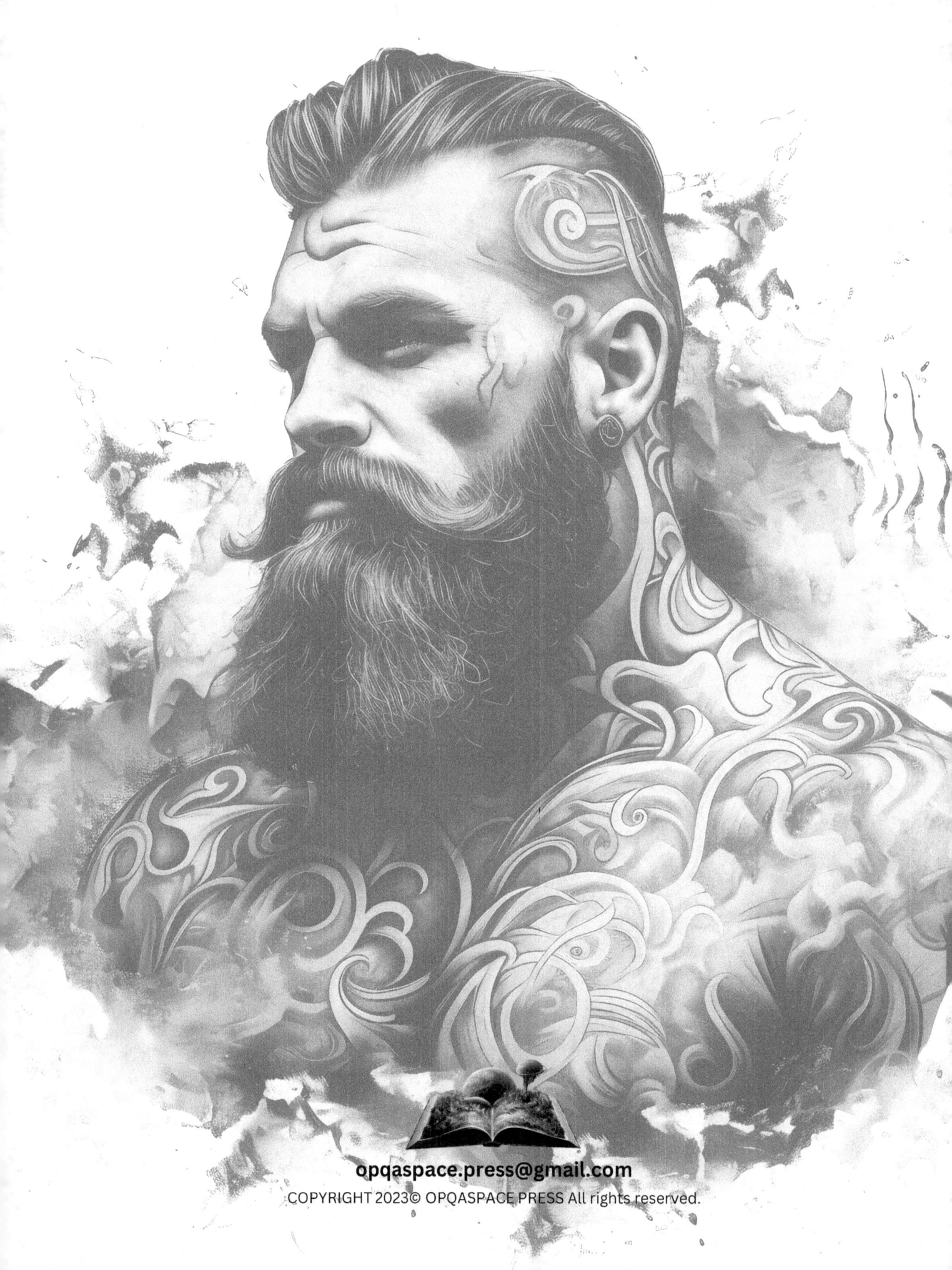

Tattoo

- A permanent mark or design made on the skin by inserting ink into the dermis layer.
- Derived from the Polynesian word "tatau", which means to mark or strike.

Meaning

- The significance or interpretation attributed to something, often influenced by personal, cultural, or symbolic associations.
- In Tattoo Art: Refers to the deeper significance behind a tattoo design, reflecting personal beliefs, values, experiences, or cultural symbolism.

Symbolism

- The use of symbols to represent ideas, qualities, or entities.
- In Tattoo Art: Refers to the symbolic representations embedded within a tattoo design, conveying deeper meanings beyond the visual aesthetics. Symbolism can vary across cultures, traditions, and personal interpretations.

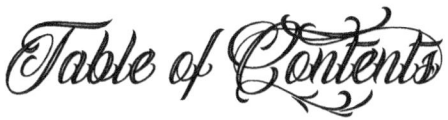

Table of Contents

Introduction:

The Power of Tattoos — Discover the profound and transformative world of tattoos in "The Power of Tattoos." Explore the captivating history, symbolism, and artistic expression behind these remarkable body art forms. From ancient traditions to modern interpretations, this introduction sets the stage for an extraordinary journey through the intersection of art, identity, and personal narratives. Prepare to be inspired by the stories etched onto the canvas of the human body, celebrating the resilience, masculinity, and self-discovery found within.

Chapter 1:

Tribal Traditions — Journey into the roots of tattooing with a diverse selection of tribal designs. Explore ancient motifs inspired by Polynesian, Maori, and Native American cultures, paying homage to their rich histories and spiritual beliefs. Each design intricately weaves together symbols of strength, courage, and ancestral connections, offering a powerful statement of identity.

Chapter 2:

Myth and Legend — Unlock the mythical realms through captivating tattoo designs inspired by folklore and legends. From Norse gods like Odin and Thor to Greek heroes such as Hercules, these designs encapsulate the heroic and larger-than-life qualities associated with these epic figures. Let these tattoos tell tales of valor, wisdom, and triumph, adding a touch of mythical splendor to the wearer's skin.

Chapter 3:

The Wild Frontier — Embark on a wild adventure with tattoo designs celebrating the spirit of the great outdoors. Inspired by the untamed beauty of nature, this chapter showcases designs featuring majestic animals like wolves, bears, and eagles. Incorporate elements such as rugged landscapes, wilderness scenes, and camping imagery to evoke a sense of freedom, strength, and connection to the natural world.

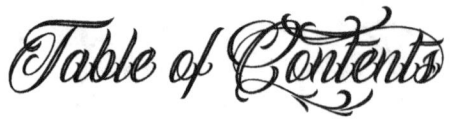

Table of Contents

Chapter 4:
Modern Masculinity – Delve into the realm of contemporary tattoo artistry with sleek and sophisticated designs. From geometric patterns to minimalist aesthetics, these tattoos blend clean lines, precise shading, and negative space to create visually striking compositions. Incorporate modern symbols such as anchors, compasses, and gears, signifying strength, resilience, and a sense of adventure.

Chapter 5:
The Spirit Within – Enter the realm of spiritual tattoos, exploring designs inspired by Eastern philosophies, sacred geometry, and mystical symbols. These designs invite introspection and inner growth, fostering a connection between body, mind, and soul. Incorporate mandalas, lotus flowers, and spiritual mantras, allowing the tattoos to serve as a constant reminder of personal transformation and enlightenment.

Conclusion:
Culmination of this captivating journey through the realm of men's tattoo designs. Embrace inked artistry as an extension of your identity, symbolizing strength, resilience, and authentic self-expression. Let your tattoos forever embody limitless potential.

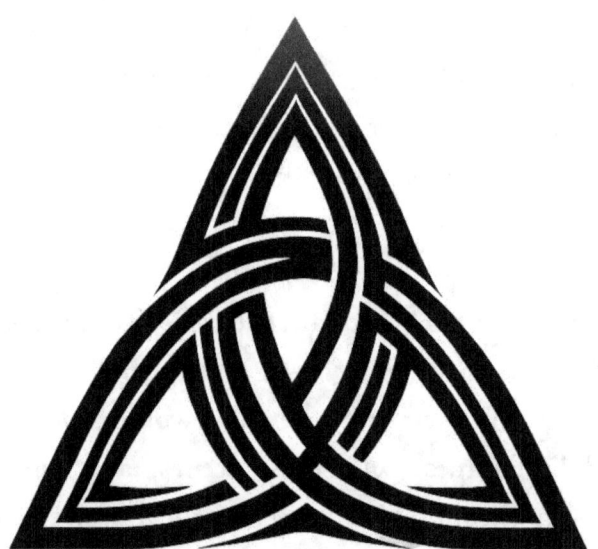

The triquetra tattoo symbolizes the interconnectedness of three elements, typically representing the concept of unity, balance, and the eternal cycle of life.

Tattoo Designs Book for Men

Meaning and Symbolism in Tattoo Art

The Power of Tattoos

In the realm of body art, tattoos have long been a powerful means of self-expression, embodying narratives, beliefs, and personal journeys. Each stroke of the tattoo needle carries the weight of stories, transforming the canvas of the human body into a living masterpiece. Tattoos transcend mere ink and skin, they become a part of who we are, speaking volumes about our identities, passions, and aspirations. They are symbols of empowerment, rebellion, and connection.

Tattoos have an ancient history, deeply rooted in various cultures across the world. From the intricate tribal designs etched on the skin of Polynesian warriors to the intricate symbols adorning the bodies of Maori and Native American tribes, tattoos have long served as a visual language, communicating tales of courage, heritage, and spirituality.

In contemporary times, tattoos have emerged as a vibrant art form, breaking free from societal stereotypes and embracing individuality. They are no longer confined to the fringes of society but have found their place in mainstream culture, captivating people from all walks of life. From athletes to musicians, actors to everyday individuals, tattoos have become a tangible expression of personal stories and beliefs.

The power of tattoos lies in their ability to transcend words, speaking directly to the soul. They are a form of rebellion against conformity, a celebration of unique identity. Tattoos are an affirmation of personal experiences, triumphs, and losses. They are a visual memoir etched onto the skin, reminding us of who we were, who we are, and who we strive to become.

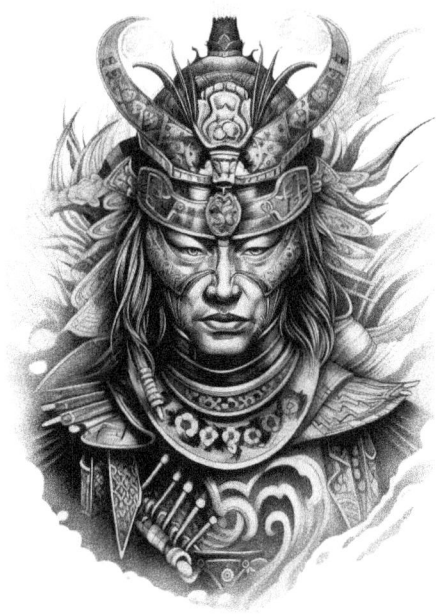

But tattoos are not merely decorative; they are laden with symbolism. Each design, line, and color carries significance, representing emotions, dreams, and connections to the world around us. Whether it's a fierce lion symbolizing strength, a delicate lotus evoking serenity, or a compass guiding us through life's uncertainties, tattoos are vessels of meaning, encapsulating the very essence of the human experience.

"Tattoo Designs Book for Men" explores the extraordinary world of tattoo designs crafted specifically for men. This anthology presents a curated collection of remarkable tattoos, showcasing the diverse stories, symbolism, and artistic prowess behind each piece. From ancient traditions to modern interpretations, tribal motifs to mythological symbols, this book celebrates the richness and power of tattoos as an art form.

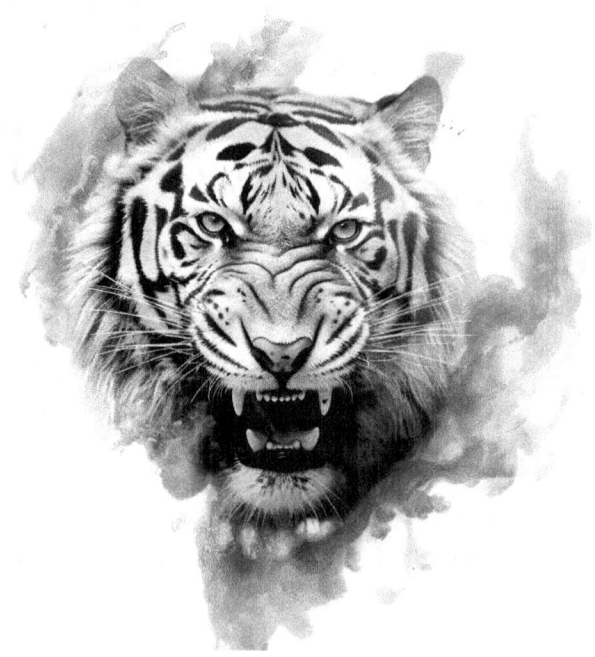

Get ready to embark on a captivating journey through inked narratives, where the skin becomes a canvas for extraordinary tales of masculinity, resilience, and self-discovery. "Tattoo Designs Book for Men" invites you to embrace the transformative power of tattoos, to dive into a world where art meets identity, and to be inspired by the remarkable stories etched onto the bodies of men.

Tribal Traditions

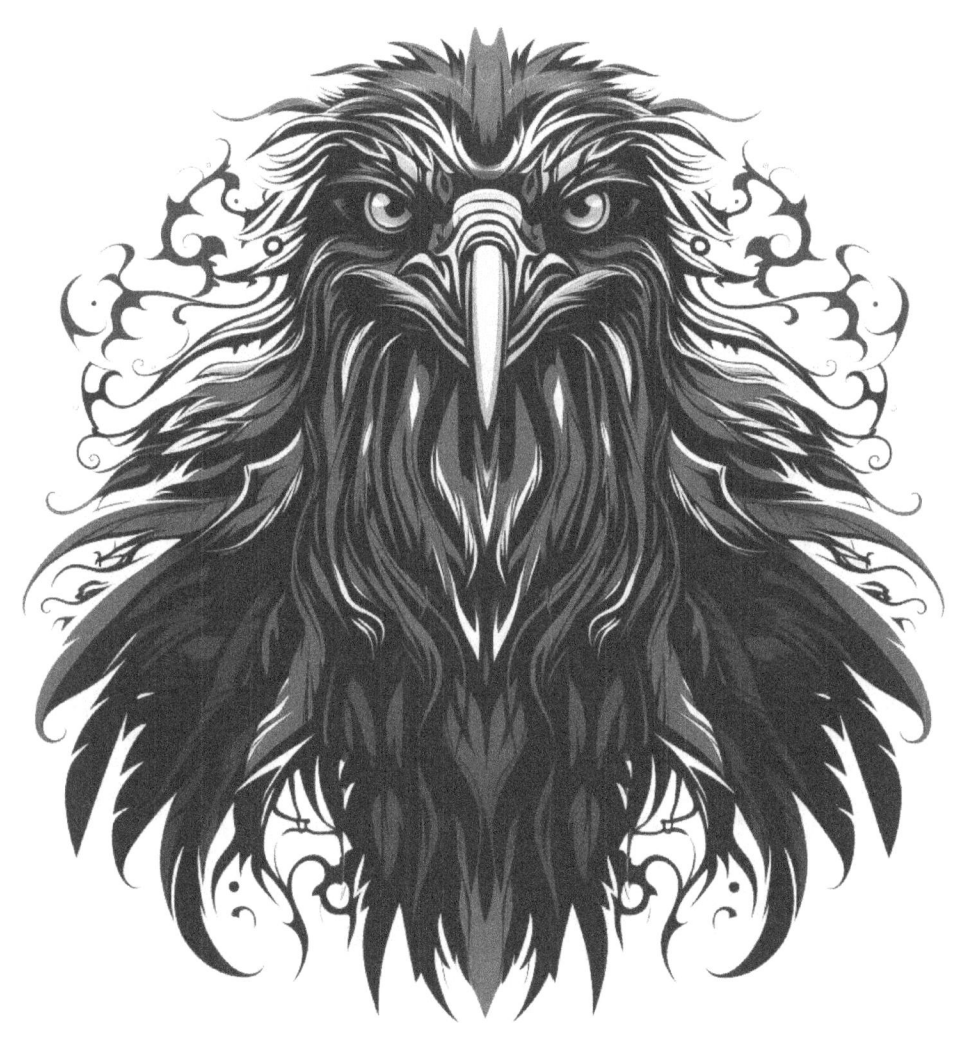

Tribal Traditions

Celebrating Ancestral Roots

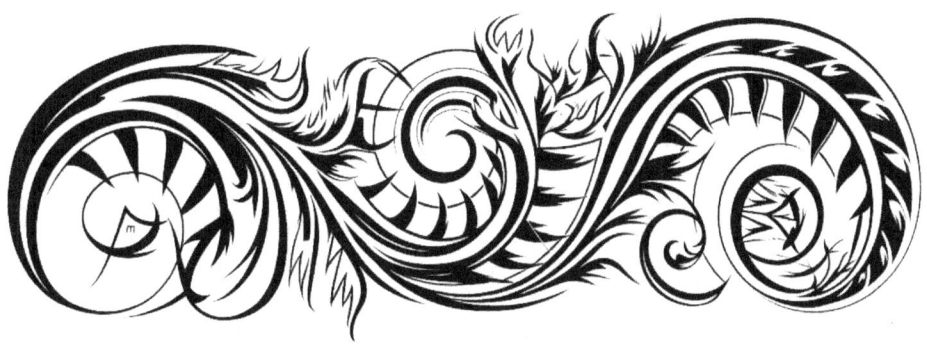

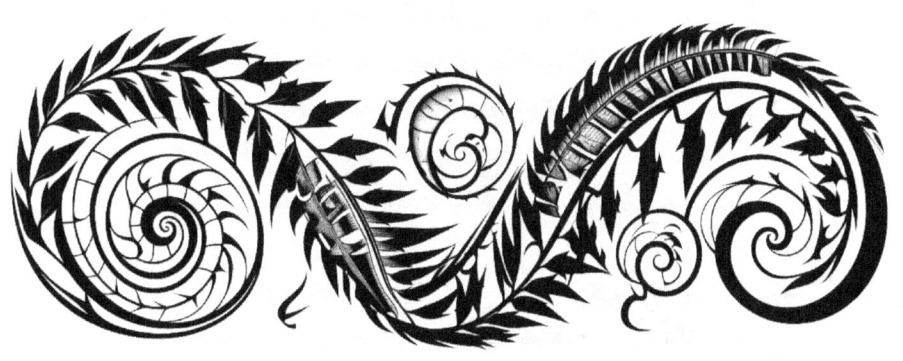

Maori-inspired Koru symbols intertwined with stylized fern leaves, symbolizing growth, renewal, and connection to nature.

Tribal Traditions

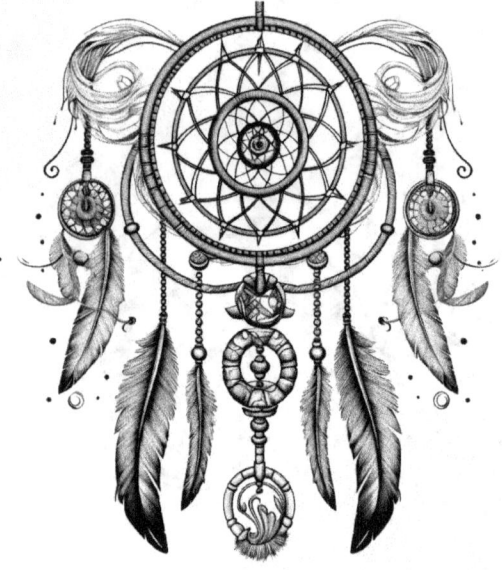

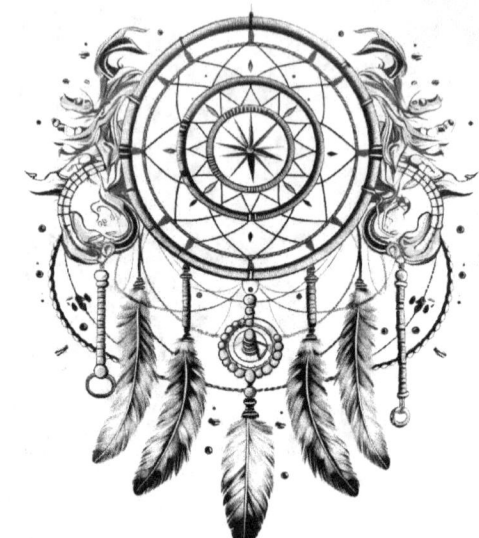

Native American dreamcatchers,
incorporating feathers, beads,
and sacred geometric patterns,
representing protection and
positive energy.

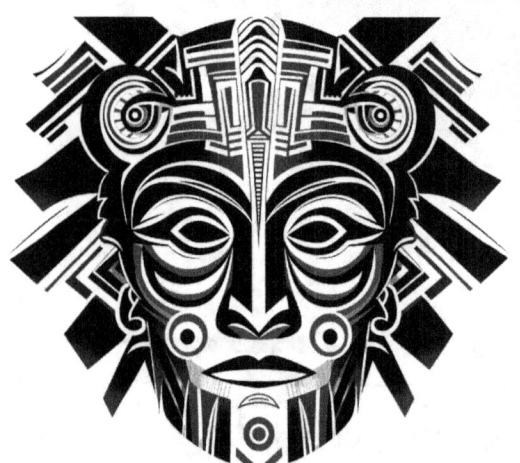

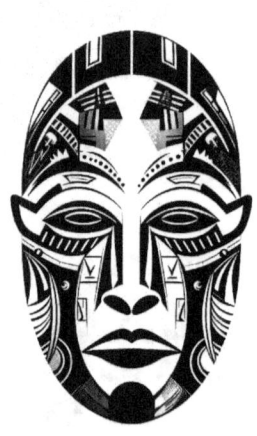

African-inspired tribal mask,
representing ancestral spirits
and cultural identity, with bold
geometric patterns.

Tribal Traditions

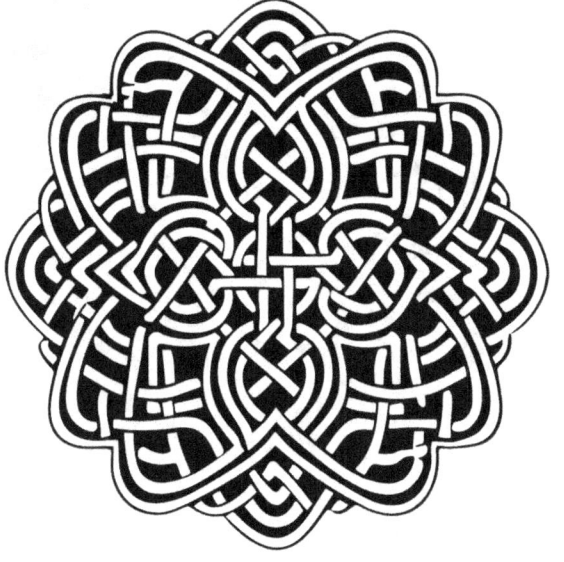

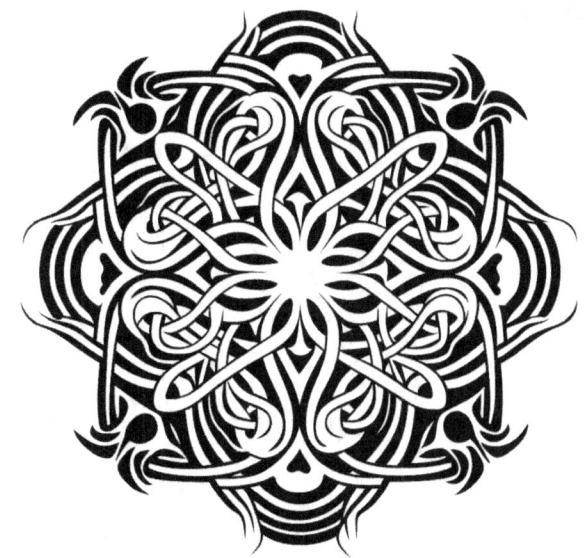

Celtic-inspired knotwork
design, intricately weaving
together endless patterns
symbolizing eternity, unity,
and interconnectedness.

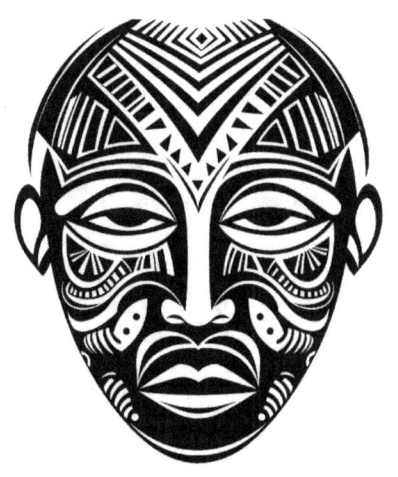

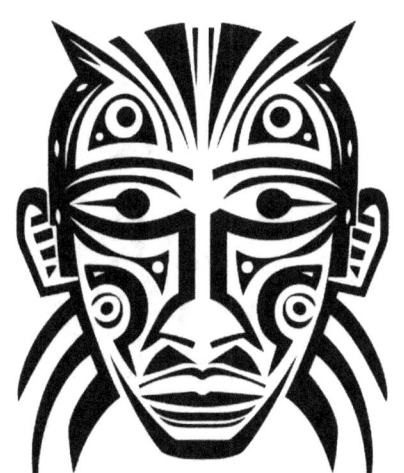

Mandinka tribal mask from
West Africa, incorporating bold
lines and patterns that
symbolize courage, strength,
and ancestral protection.

Tribal Traditions

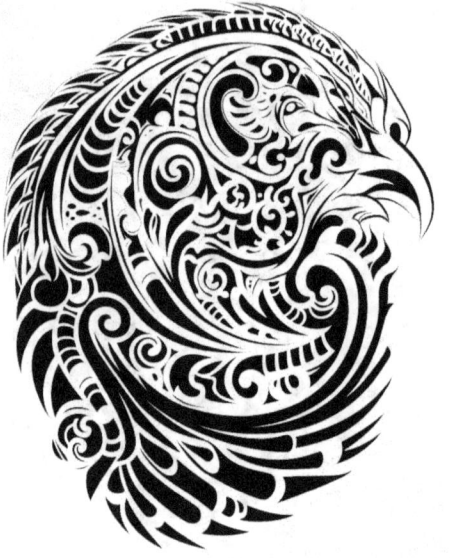

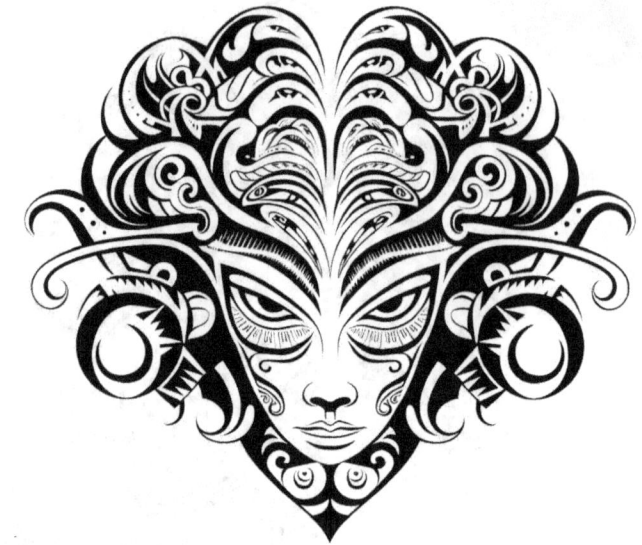

Maori-inspired manaia, a spiritual guardian figure combining elements of humans, birds, and reptiles, representing balance, protection, and spirituality.

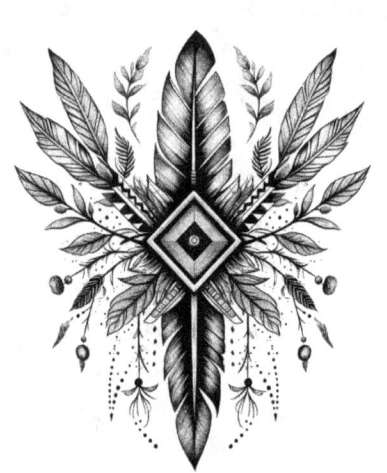

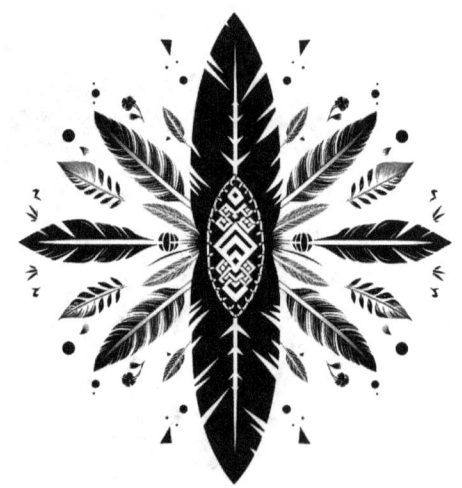

Native American-inspired arrowhead design, adorned with feathers and earthy tones, symbolizing direction, focus, and resilience.

Tribal Traditions

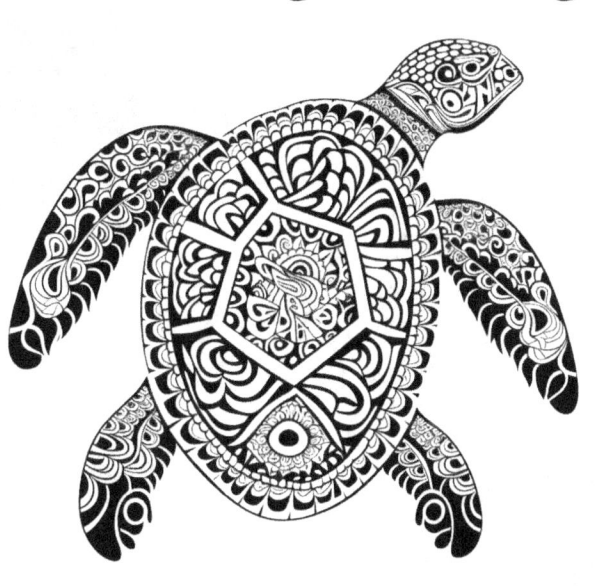

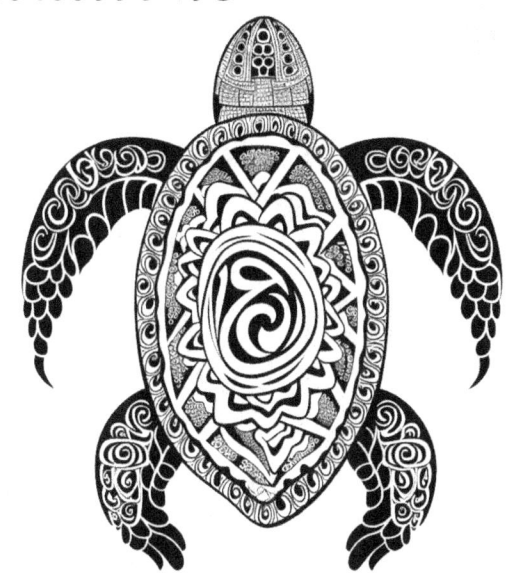

Polynesian—inspired giant turtle
design, incorporating swirling
patterns and symbols of longevity,
navigation, and family.

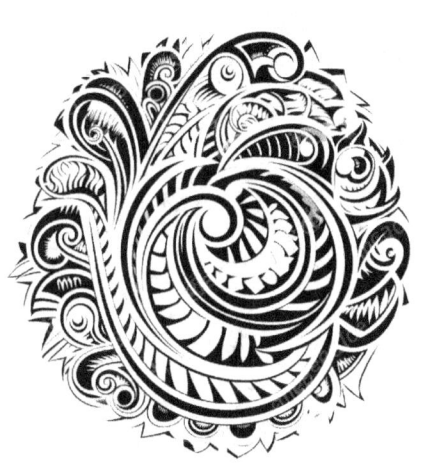

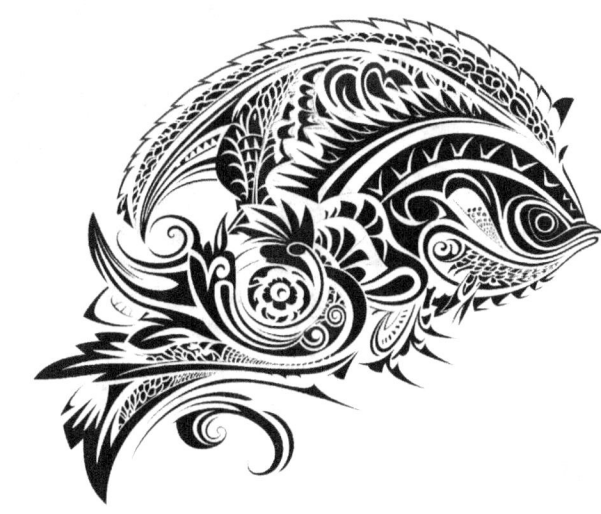

Samoan—inspired pe'a design,
incorporating intricate patterns
of shells and fish scales,
representing status, courage,
and heritage.

Tribal Traditions

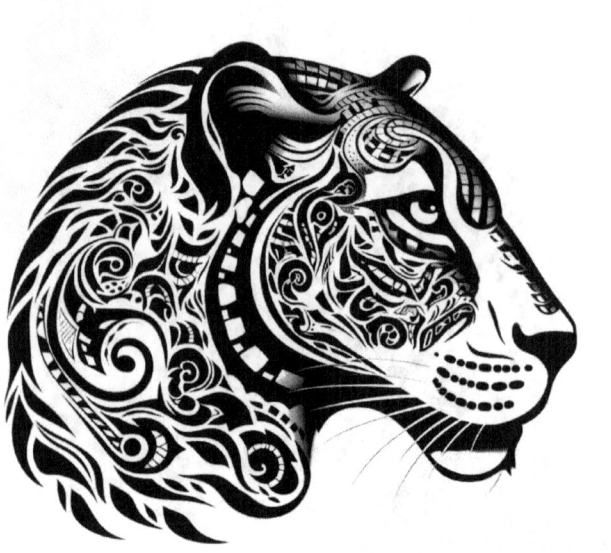

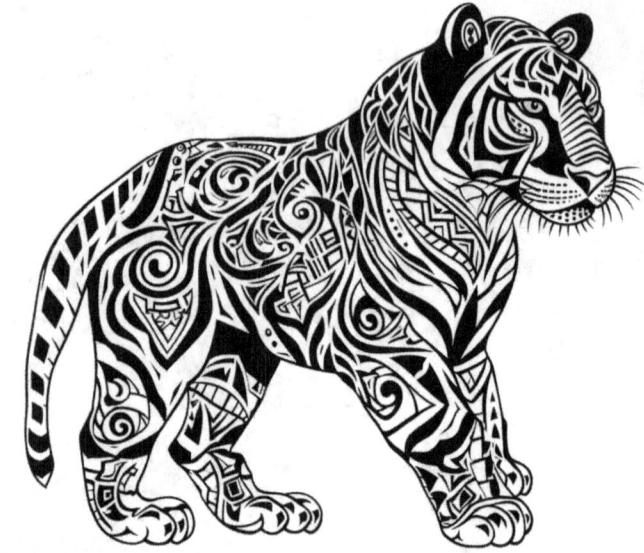

Aboriginal-inspired dot work design, depicting an intricate representation of a tiger, symbolizing strength, agility, and connection to the land.

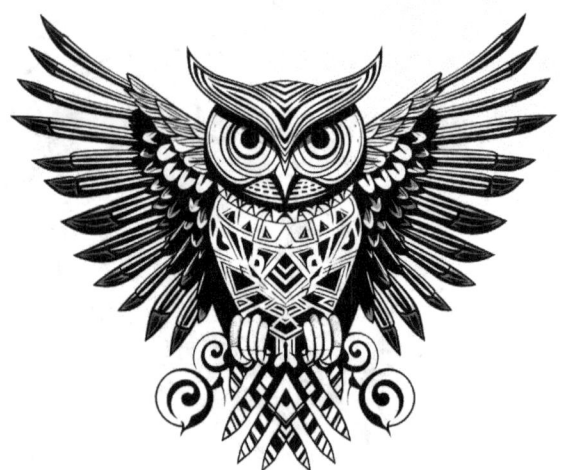

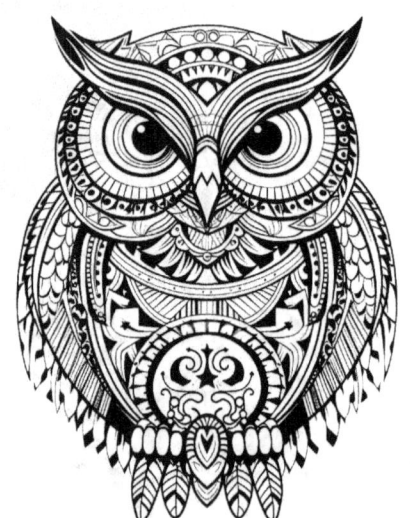

Aboriginal-inspired dot work design, depicting an intricate representation of a owl, symbolizing wisdom, focus, and connection to the family

Tribal Traditions

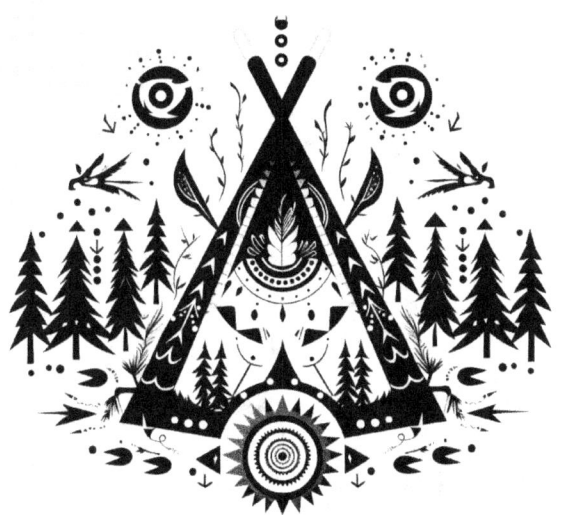

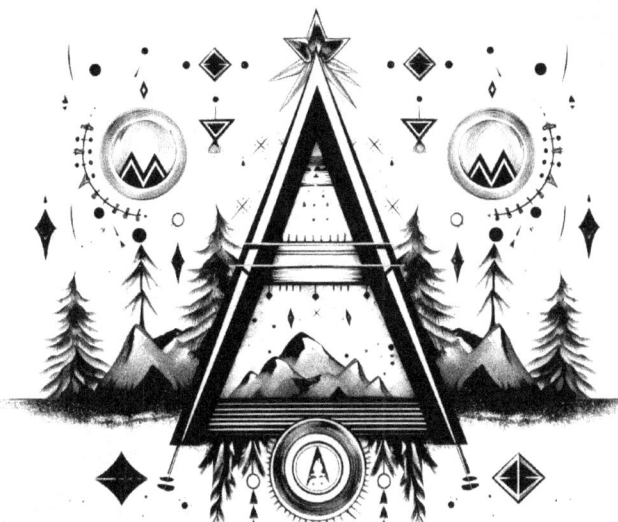

Native American tipis and tepees, representing shelter, community, and a nomadic spirit.

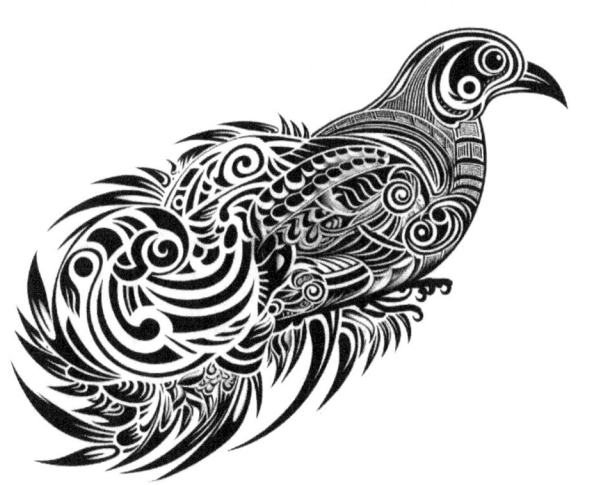

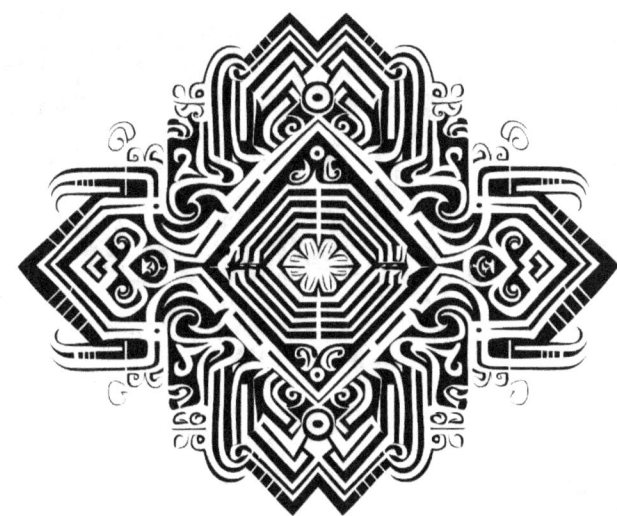

Filipino-inspired Kalinga tribal design, with flowing lines and intricate patterns inspired by nature, signifying bravery and cultural heritage.

Tribal Traditions

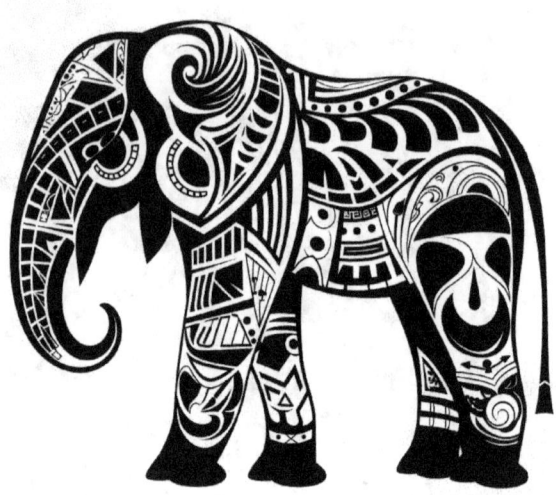 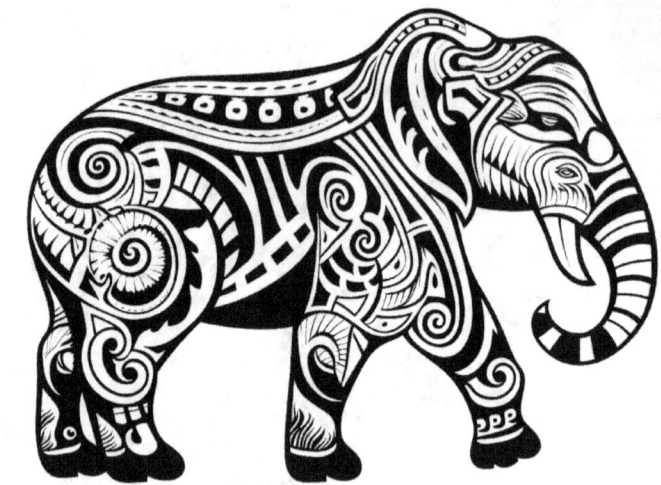

haida-inspired elephant, symbolizing strength, independence, and leadership, adorned with traditional tribal patterns and motifs.

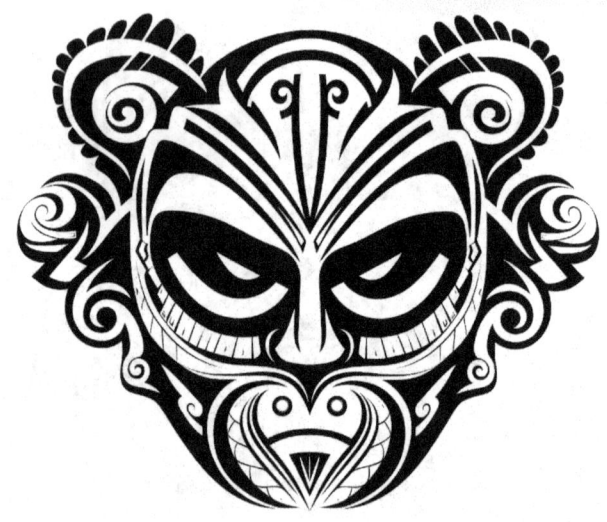 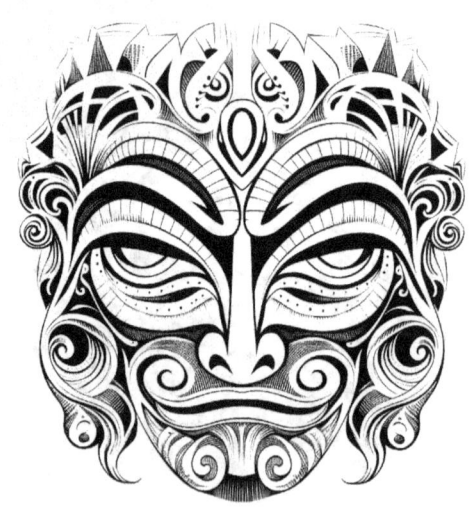

Papua New Guinean-inspired mask design, with bold lines and patterns depicting a fierce and protective guardian spirit.

Tribal Traditions

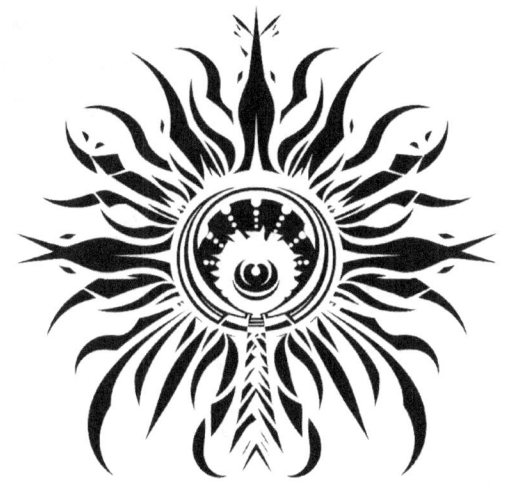

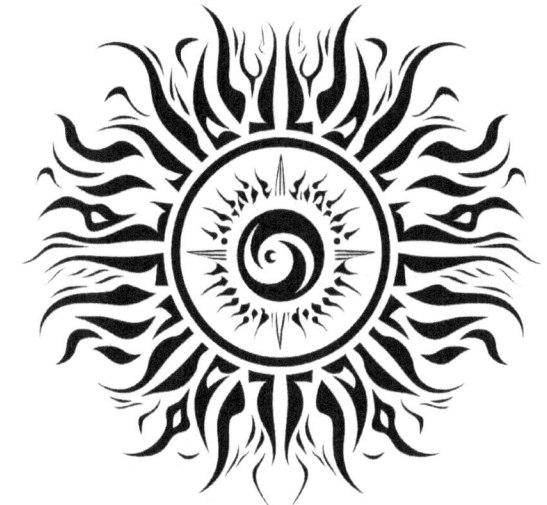

Tribal sun symbol with rays extending into tribal patterns, evoking power, vitality, and a connection to the celestial forces.

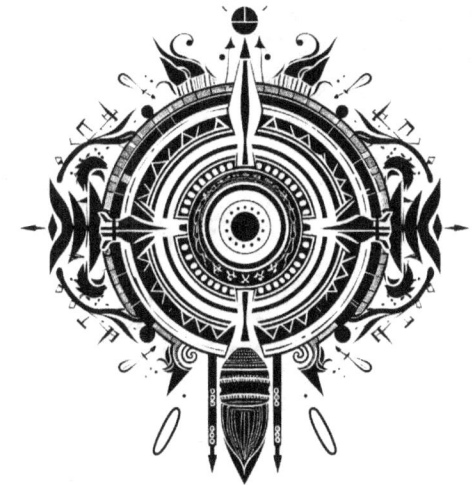

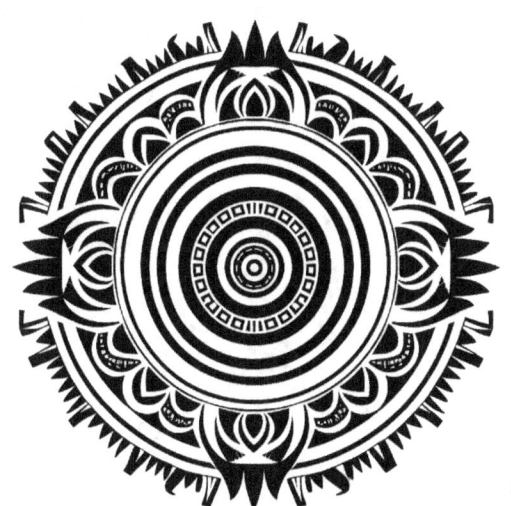

Ethiopian-inspired tribal pattern, with intricate designs inspired by Ethiopian tribes such as the hamar, symbolizing cultural pride and identity.

Tribal Traditions

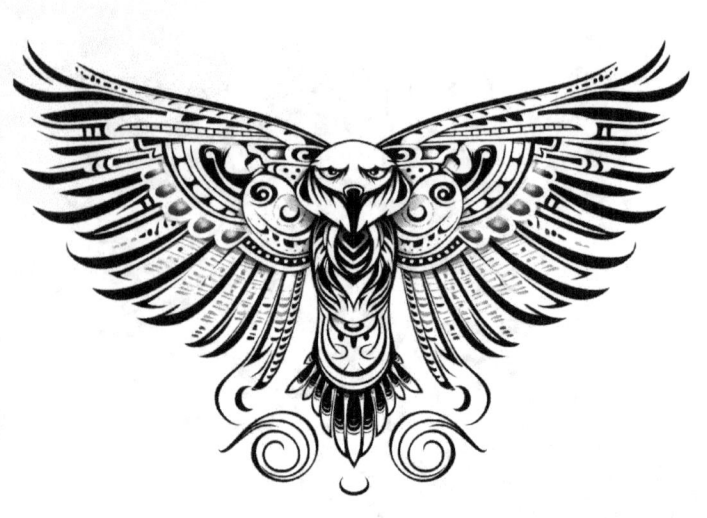

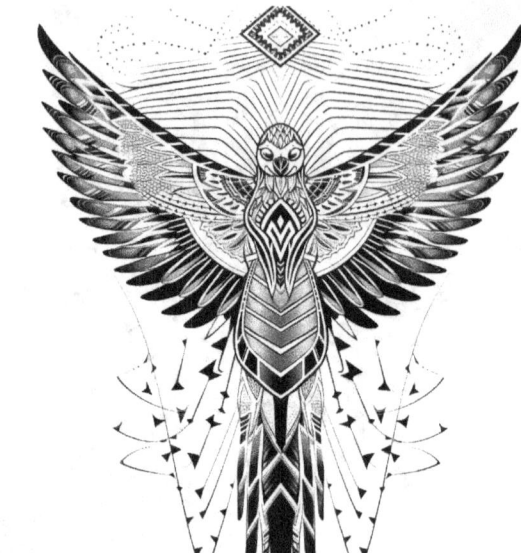

Native American-inspired thunderbird, with its outstretched wings embodying strength, protection, and spiritual energy.

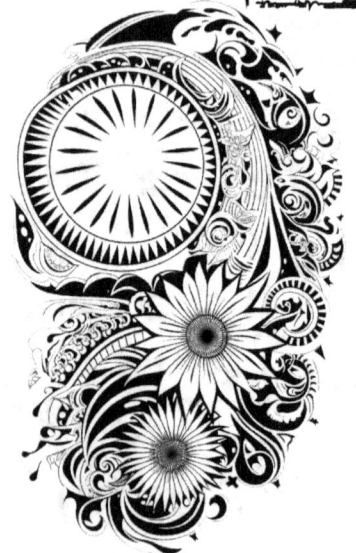

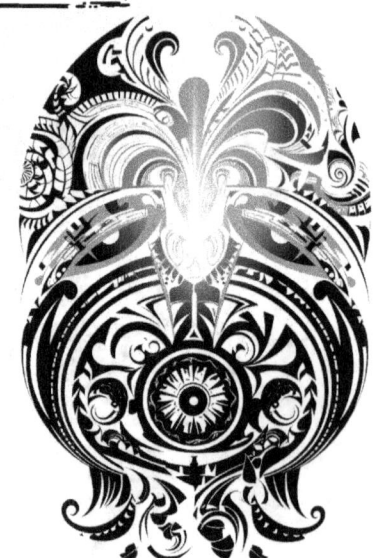

Mesmerizing combination of tribal motifs, including intricately designed ocean waves, flowers, and a stylized sun.

Tribal Traditions

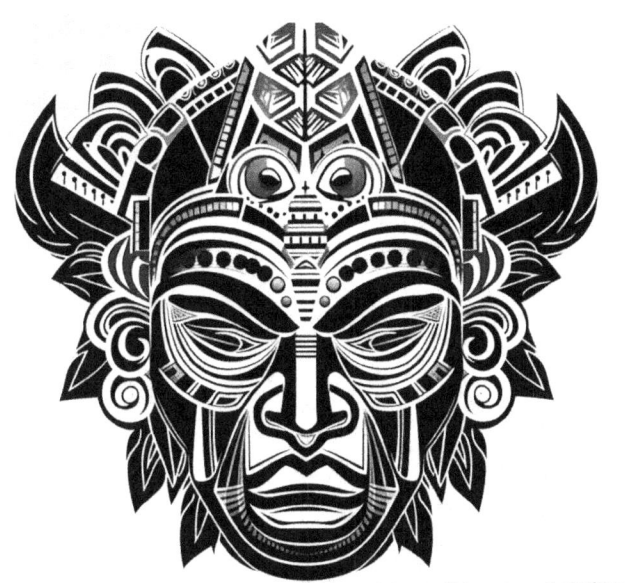

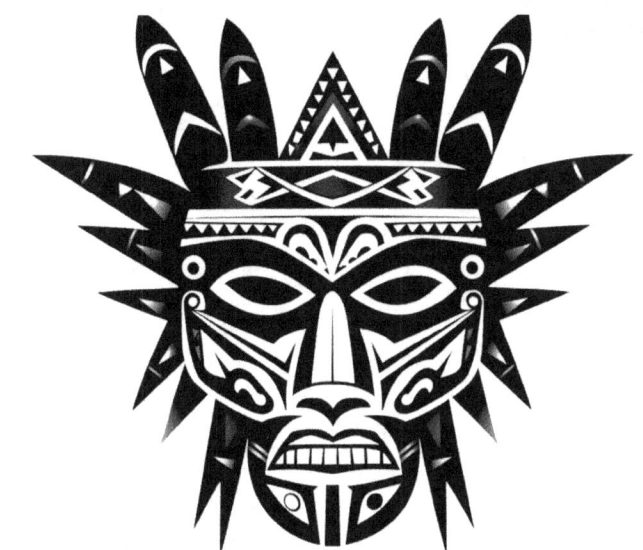

African-inspired tribal mask,
representing ancestral spirits and
cultural identity.

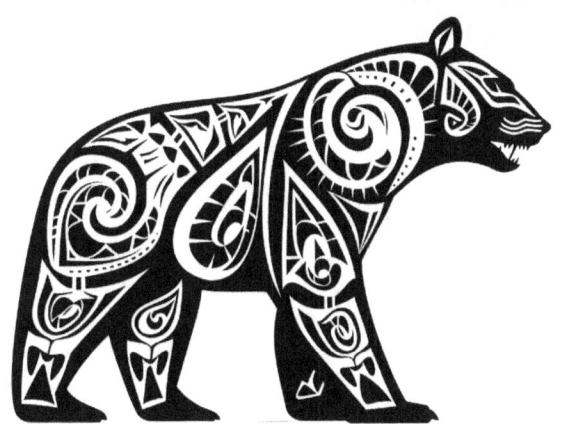

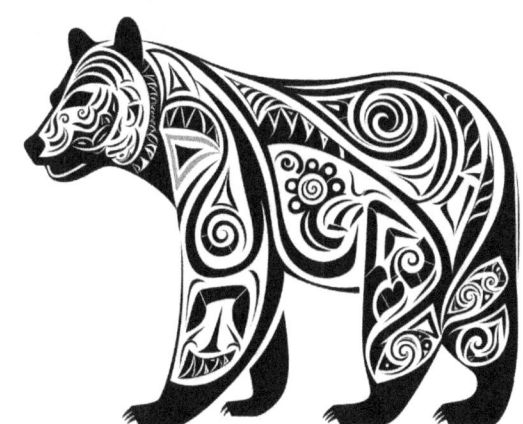

haida-inspired bear, symbolizing
strength, independence, and leadership,
adorned with traditional tribal
patterns and motifs.

Myth and Legend

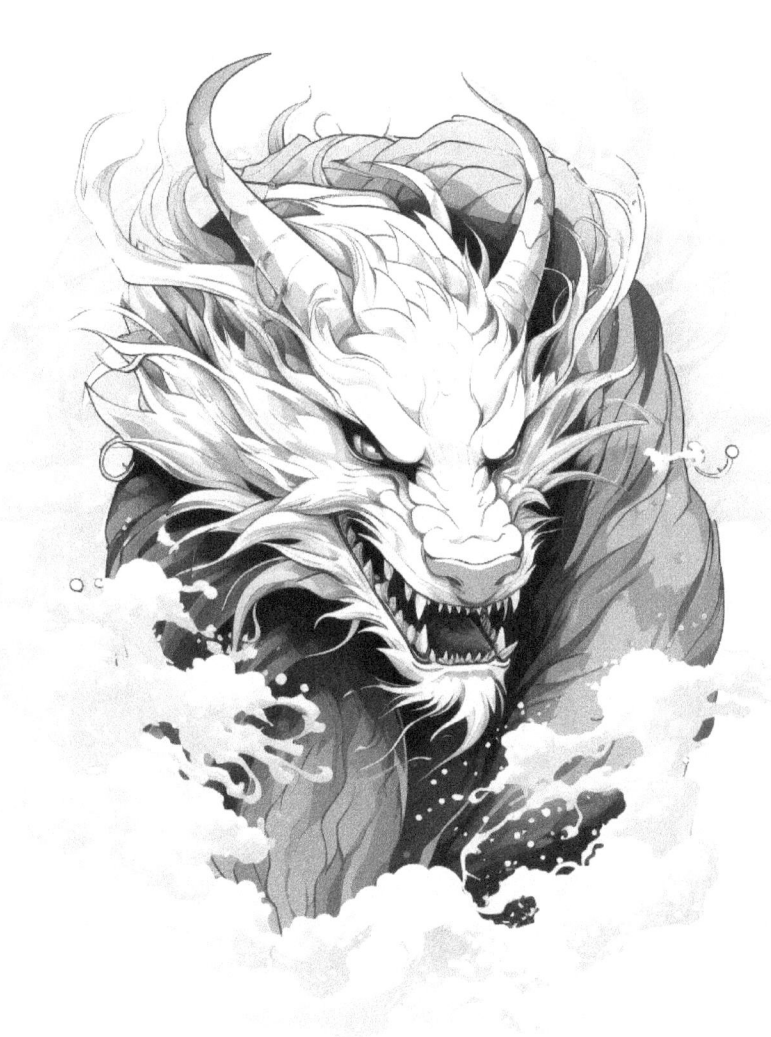

Myth and Legend
Immortalizing heroic Tales

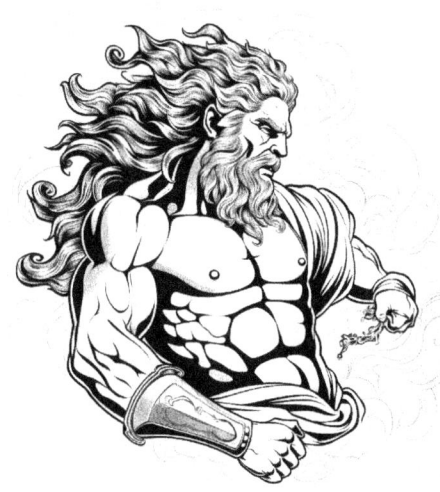

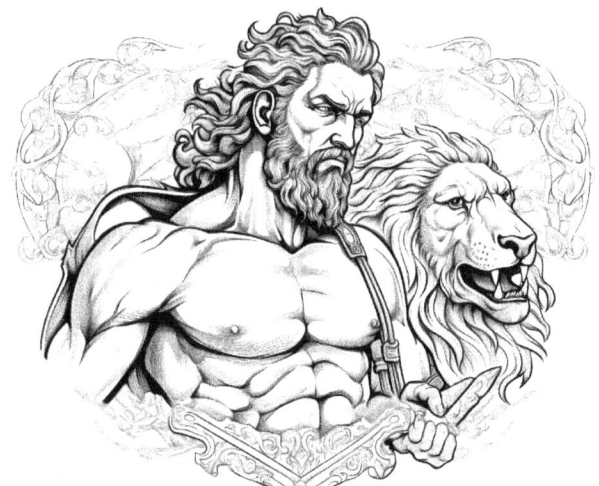

Greek hero hercules, showcasing his renowned feats, such as slaying the Nemean Lion and holding up the heavens, symbolizing strength, bravery, and overcoming challenges.

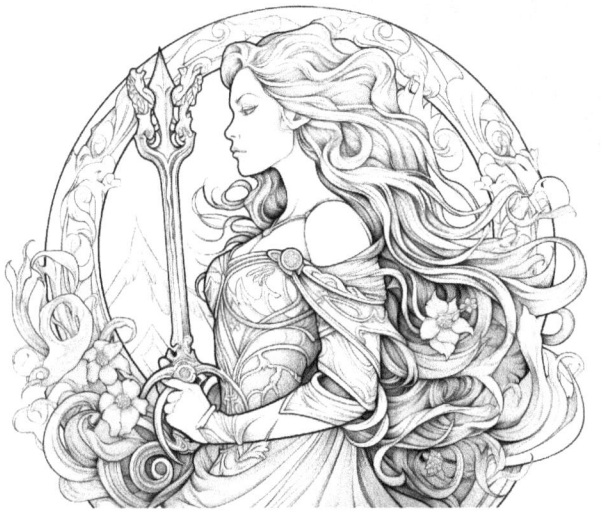

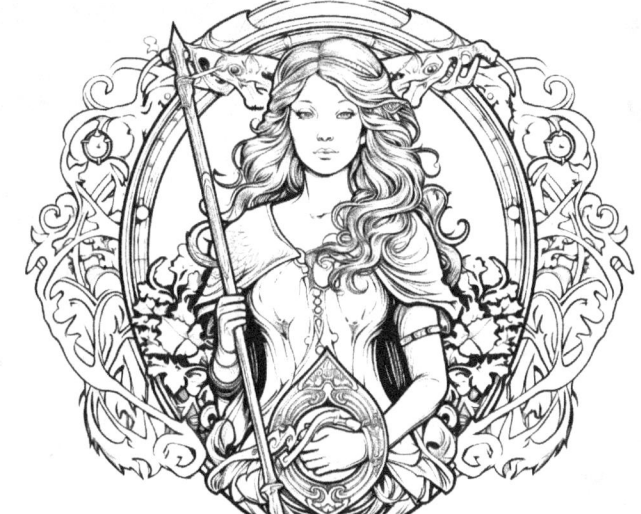

Arthurian legend of the Lady of the Lake, holding the mystical sword Excalibur, representing feminine power, mysticism, and the bestowing of destiny.

Myth and Legend

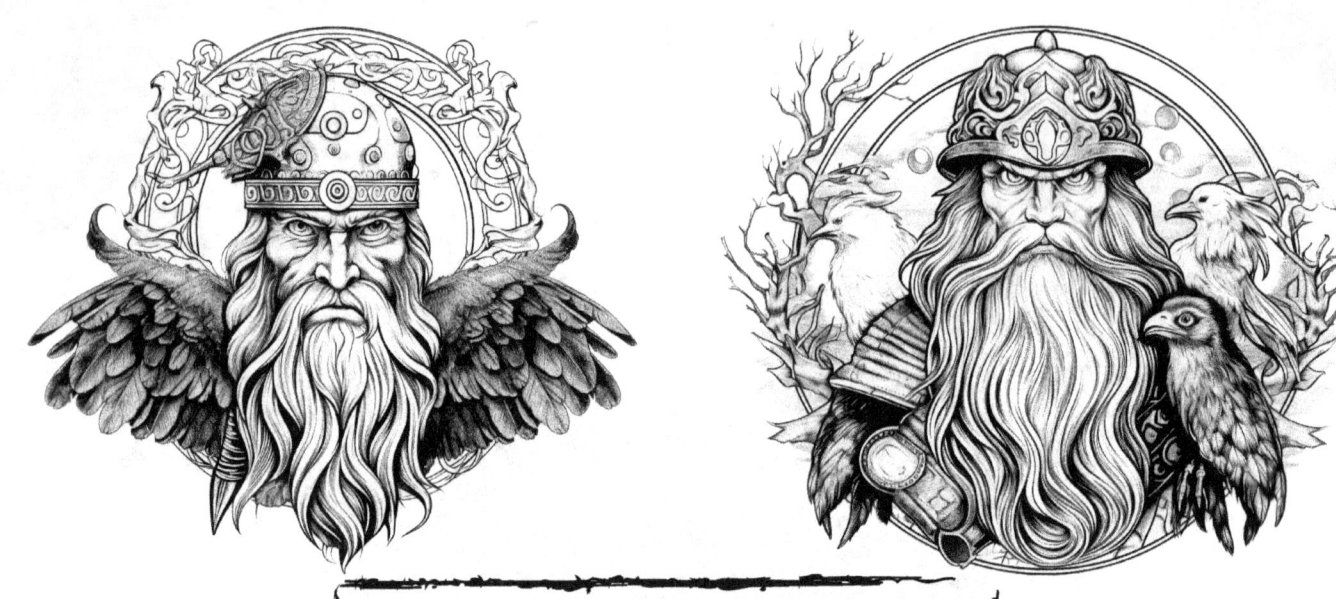

Norse god Odin, ravens and spear, symbolizing wisdom, knowledge, and the pursuit of truth.

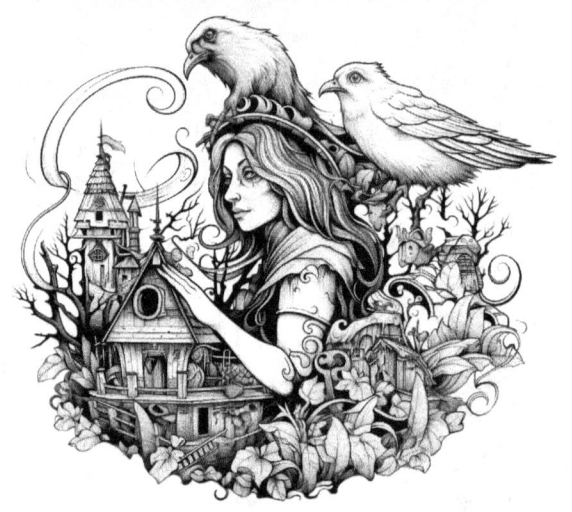

Slavic folklore character Baba Yaga, the witch with a magical hut, embodying both wisdom and danger, symbolizing the mysteries of the wild and the transformative power of nature.

Myth and Legend

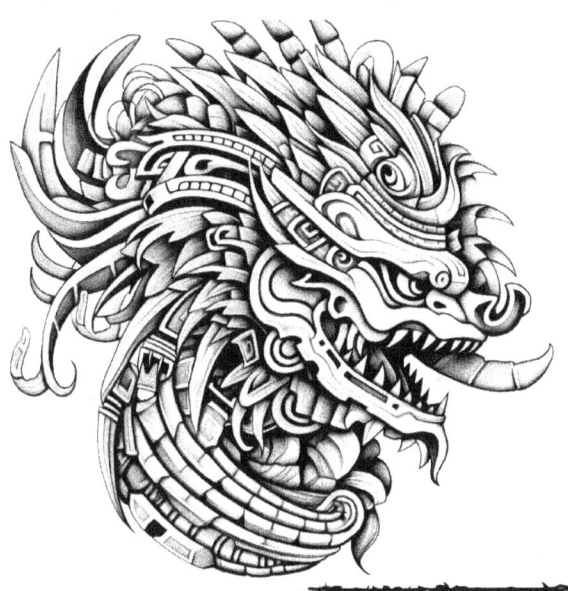

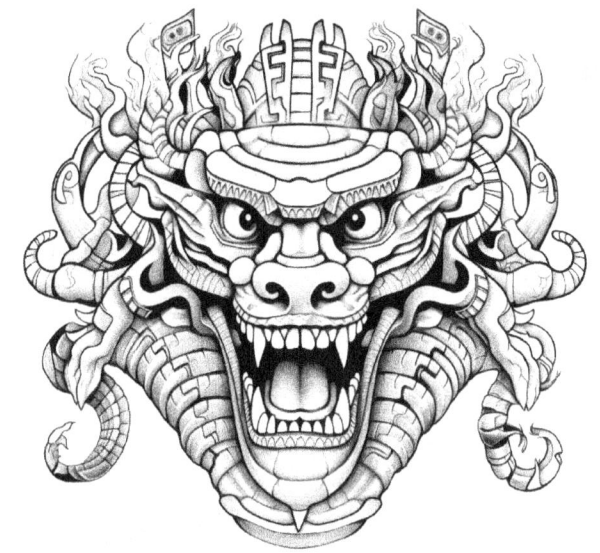

Aztec god Quetzalcoatl, a feathered serpent deity, symbolizing wisdom, fertility, and the duality of creation and destruction.

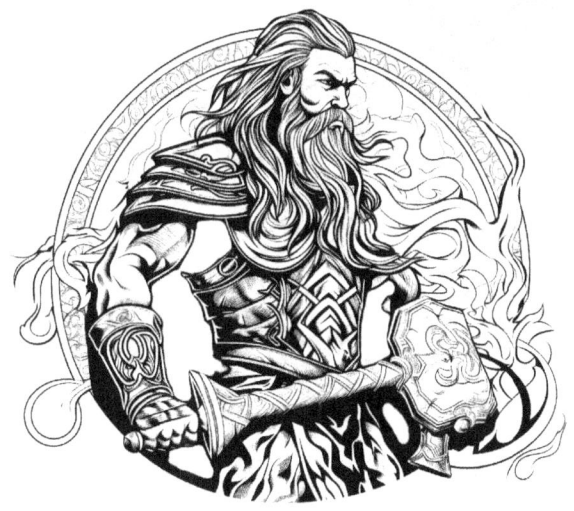

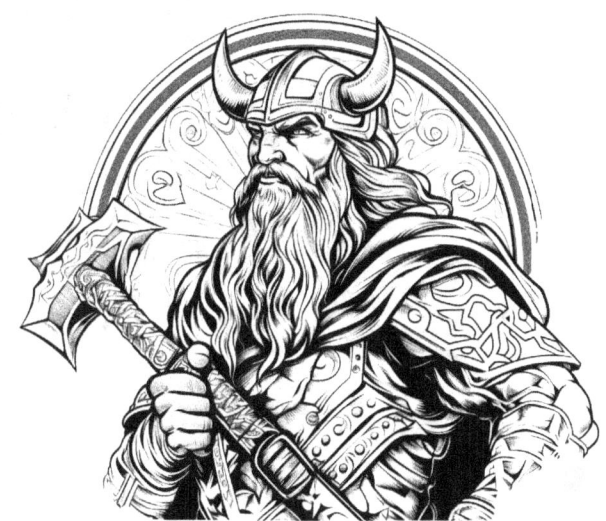

Norse god Thor, depicted with his mighty hammer, Mjölnir, held aloft, symbolizing strength, protection, and the power to ward off evil.

Myth and Legend

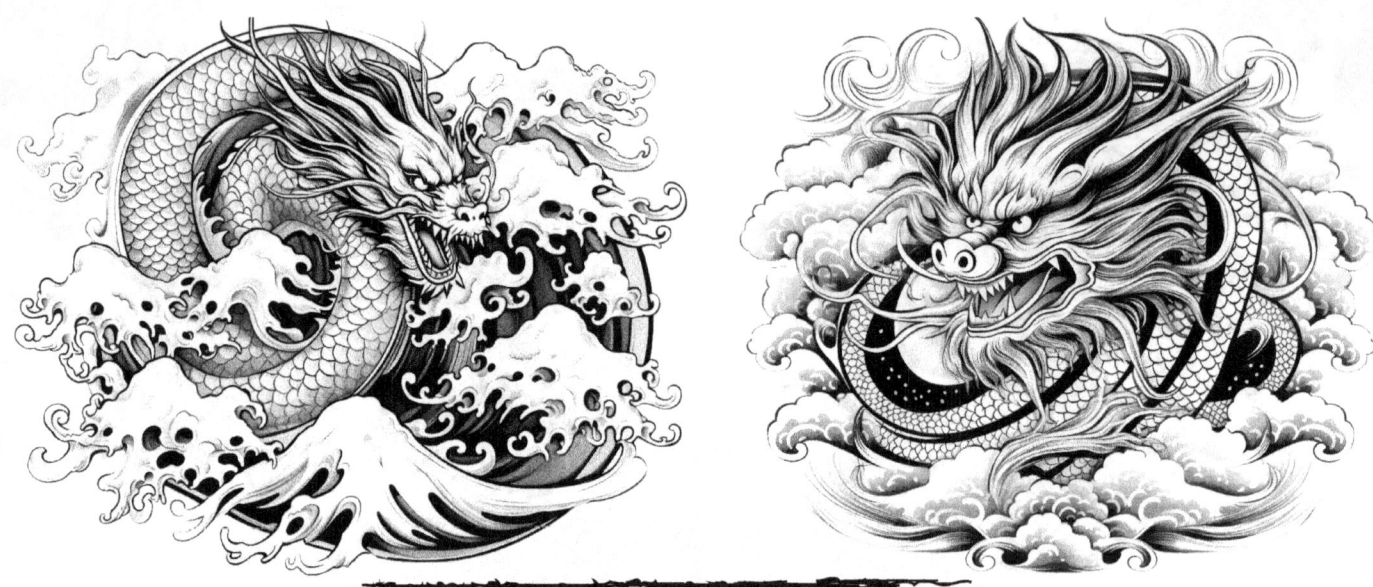

Chinese mythological creature, the Dragon, known for its strength, wisdom, and auspicious powers, intertwined with clouds and waves, symbolizing good fortune and protection.

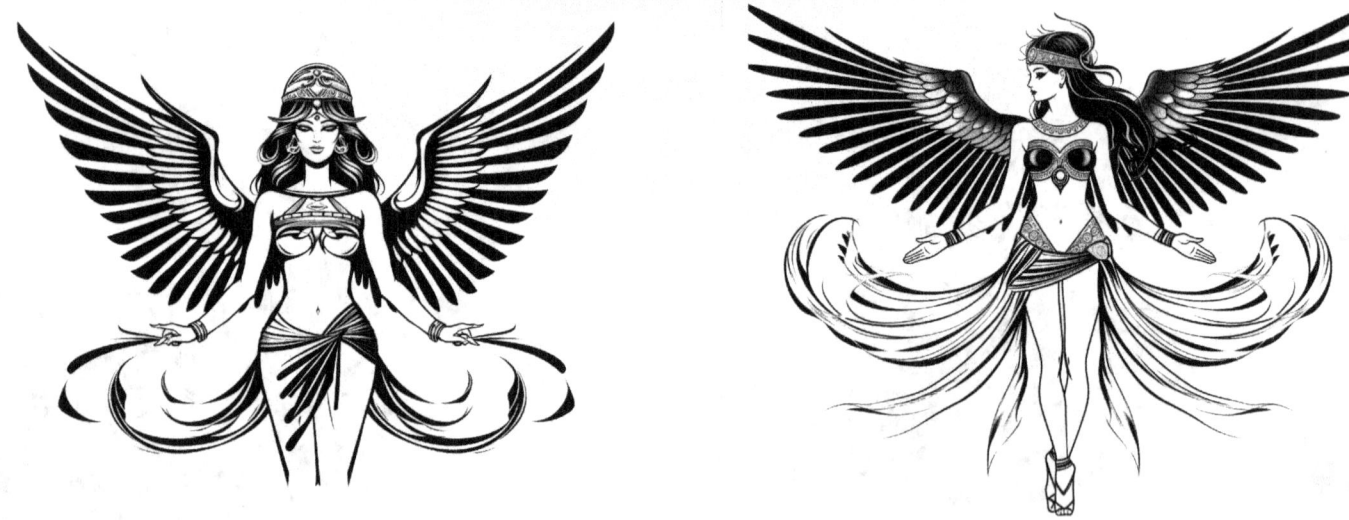

Egyptian goddess Isis with outstretched wings, symbolizing femininity, rebirth, and divine nurture.

Myth and Legend

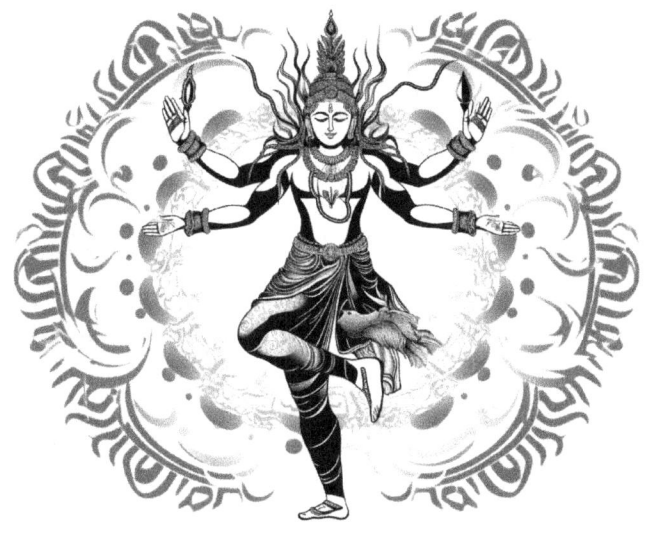

hindu god Shiva, with his multiple arms and the Nataraja dance pose, symbolizing creation, destruction, and the cosmic balance of life.

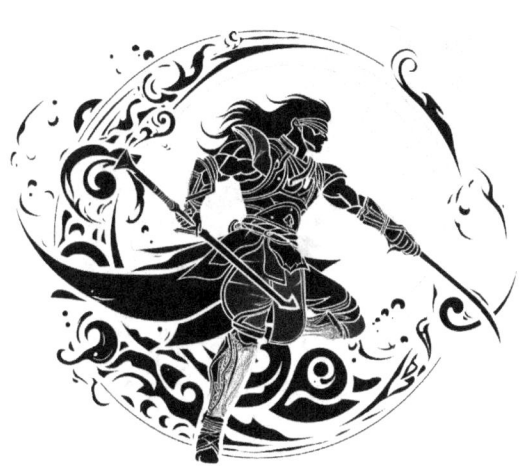

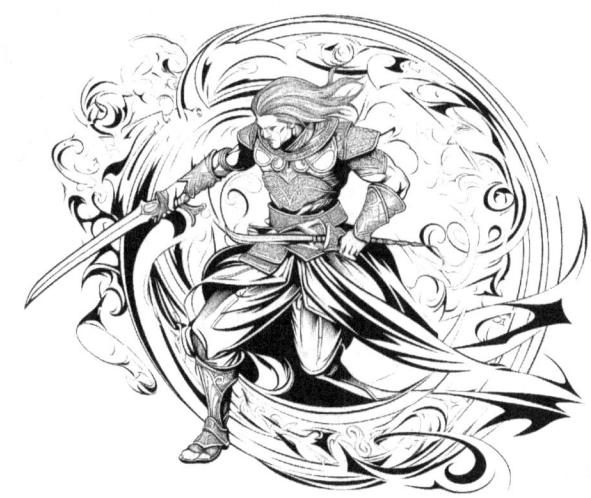

Celtic legend of Cú Chulainn, with his mighty spear and the warp spasm, representing bravery, ferocity, and the hero's journey.

Myth and Legend

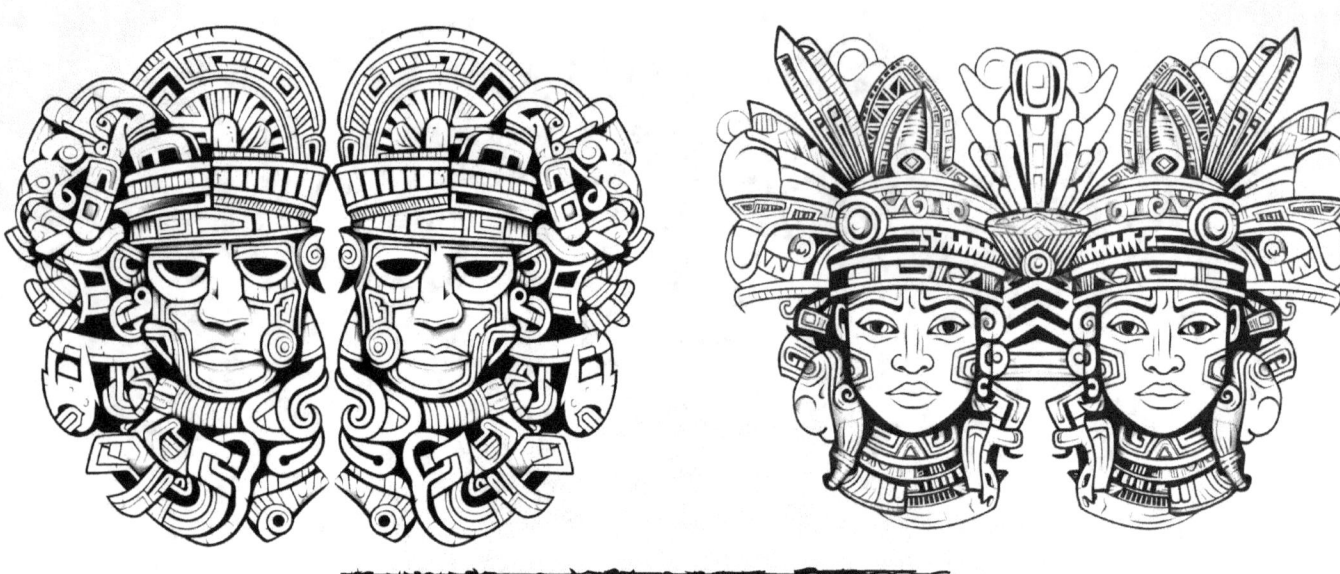

Mayan legend of the hero Twins, hunahpu and Xbalanque, on their journey through the underworld, representing bravery, resilience, and triumph over adversity.

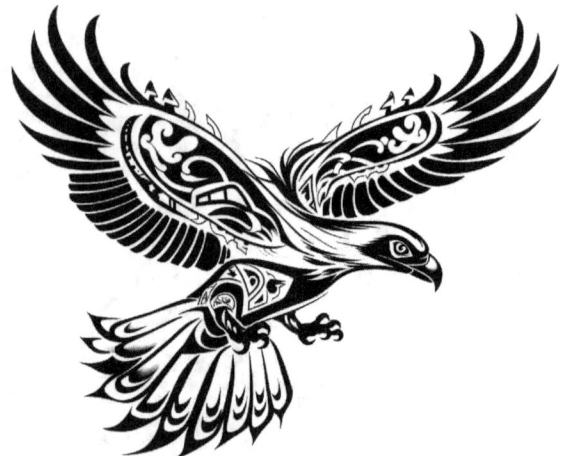

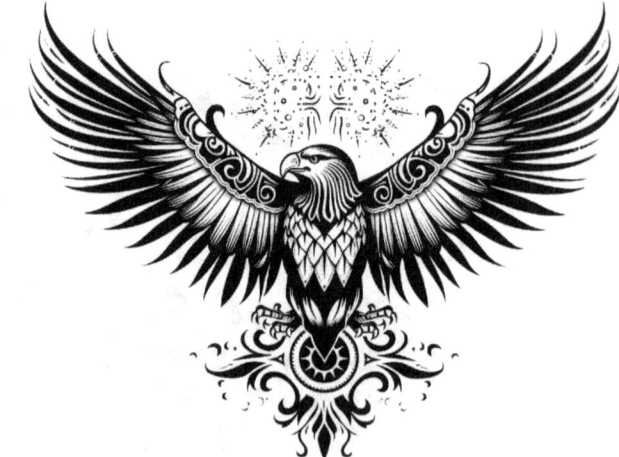

Native American legend of the Thunderbird, a powerful avian spirit associated with thunder and lightning, symbolizing strength, protection, and divine energy.

Myth and Legend

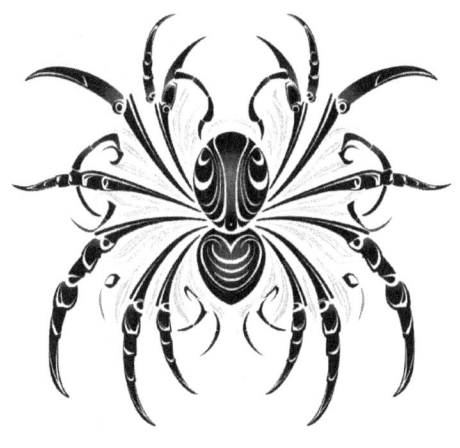 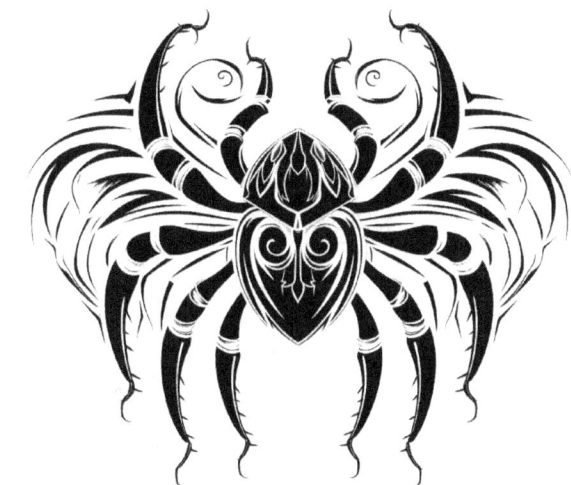

African folktale character Anansi the Spider, known for his cunning and trickery, symbolizing wisdom, storytelling, and the importance of wit.

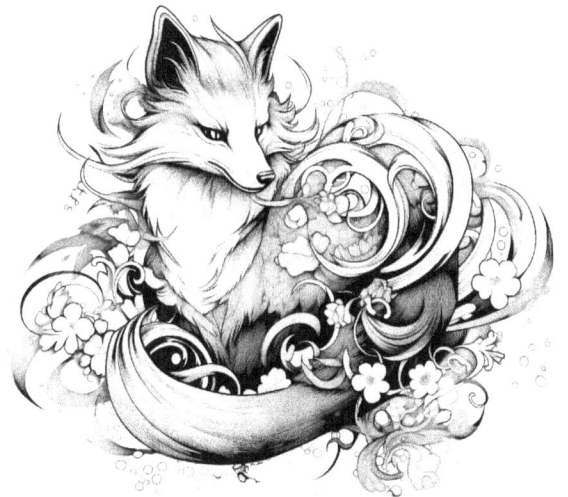 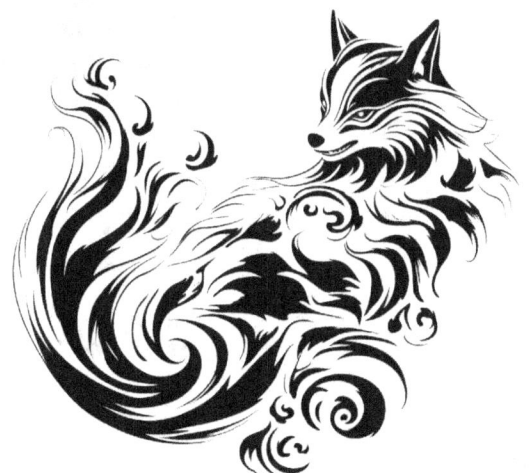

Japanese folklore creature, the Kitsune, a fox with multiple tails, representing intelligence, trickery and shape-shifting abilities.

Myth and Legend

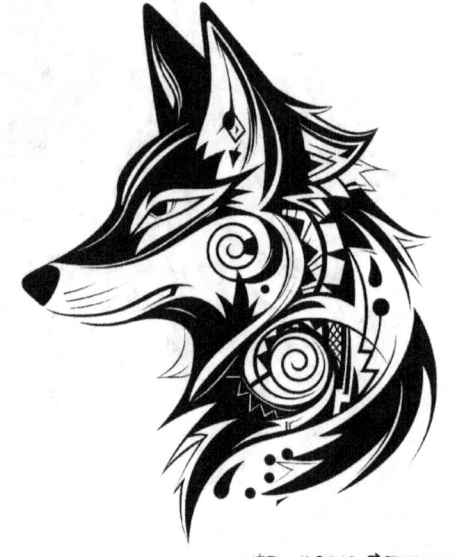

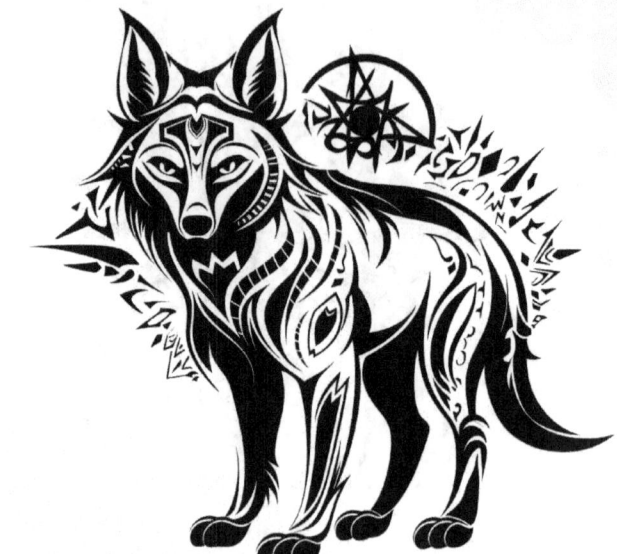

Native American legend of the Trickster Coyote, known for his mischief and cleverness, symbolizing adaptability, resourcefulness, and the lessons learned from life's challenges.

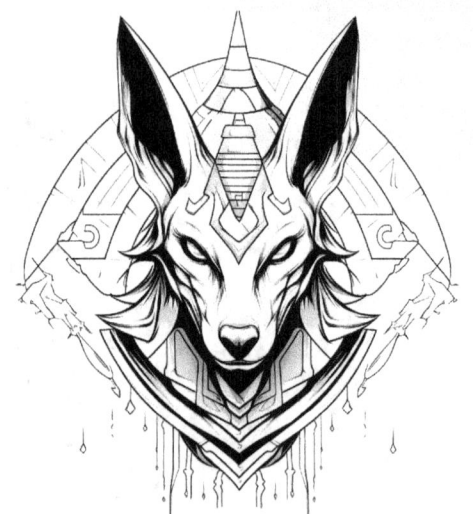

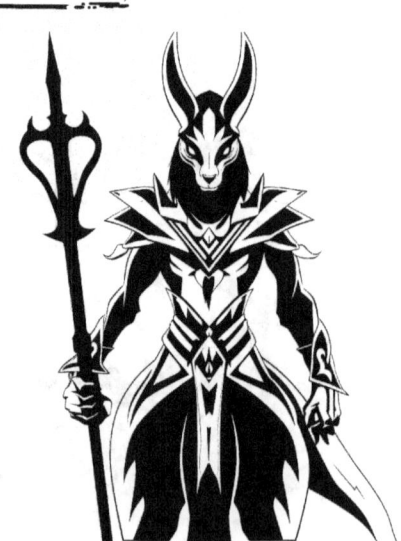

Egyptian god Anubis, the jackal-headed deity of the afterlife, embodying protection, guidance, and the passage into the realm of the dead.

Myth and Legend

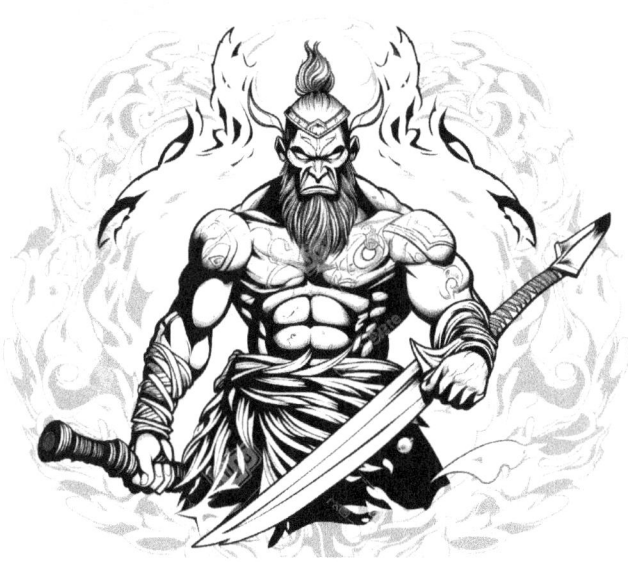

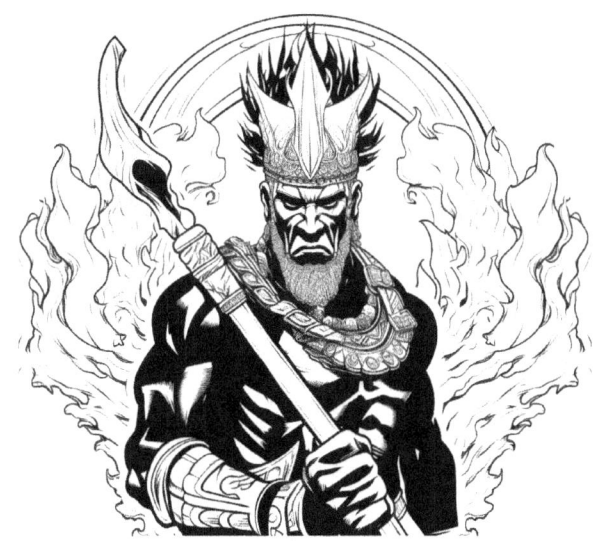

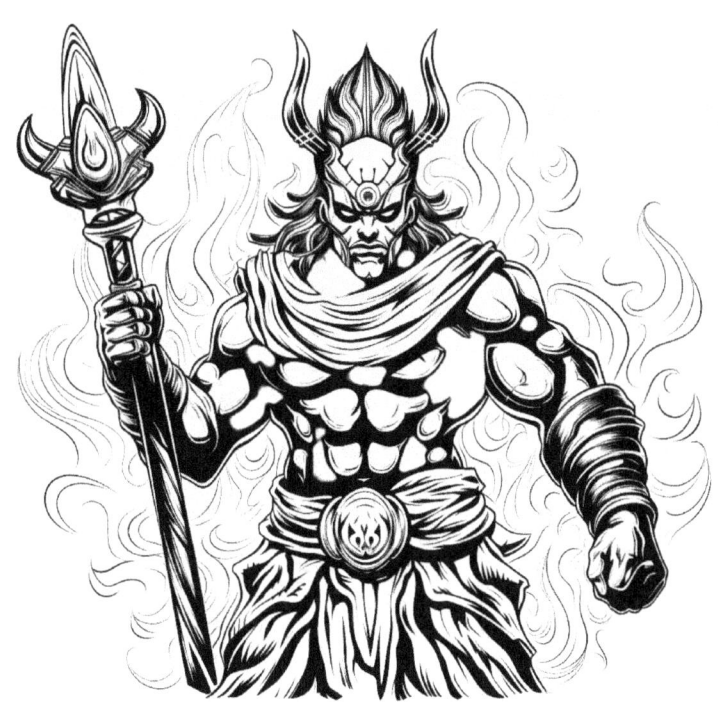

African deity Ogun, the god of war and iron, depicted with a machete and surrounded by flames, symbolizing courage, determination, and forging one's own path.

The Wild Frontier

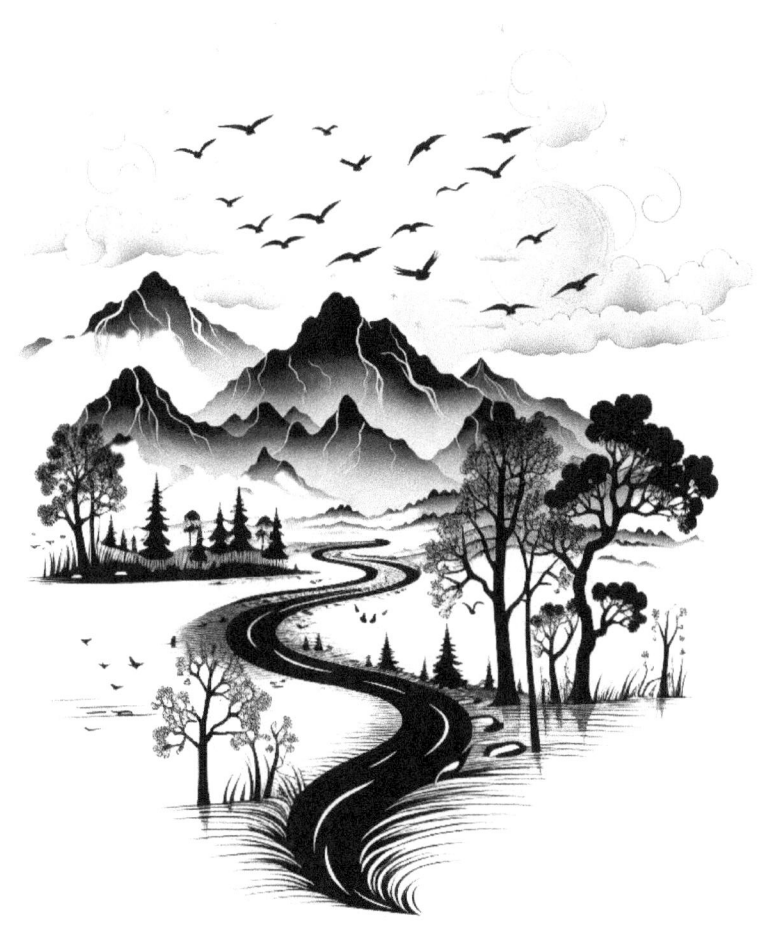

The Wild Frontier
Embracing Nature's Majesty

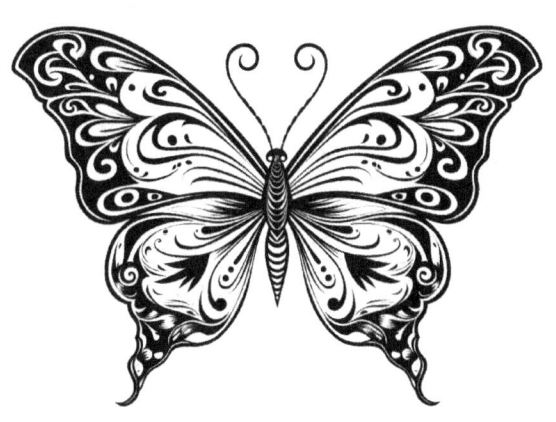 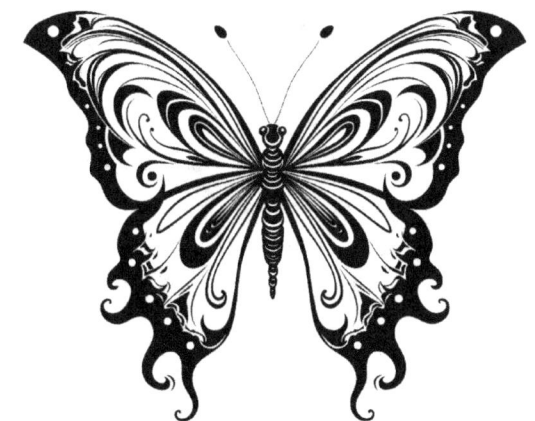

Delicate beauty of a butterfly,
symbolizing transformation, grace, and
the fleeting nature of life.

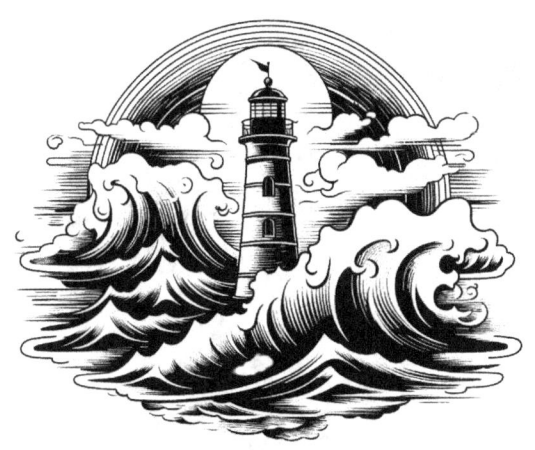 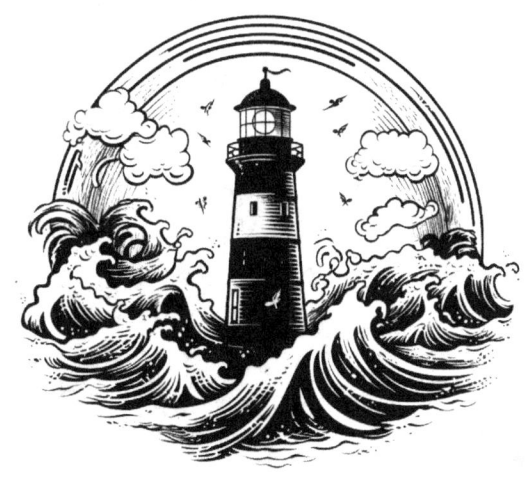

Essence of the ocean with crashing
waves and a lighthouse, symbolizing
adventure, guidance, and the journey
through life's challenges.

The Wild Frontier

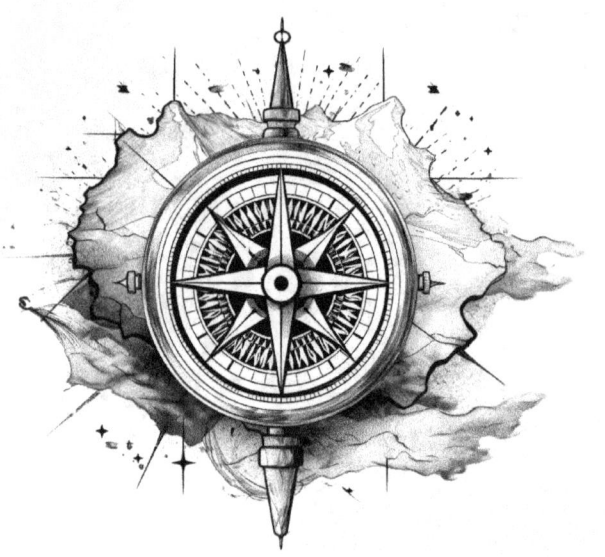

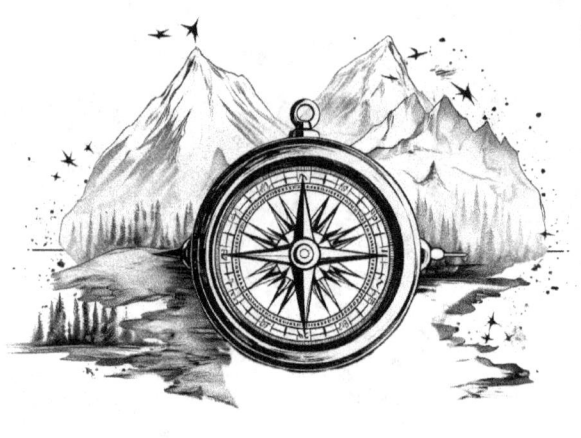

Spirit of adventure with a compass and a vintage map, symbolizing a love for exploration and the call of the unknown.

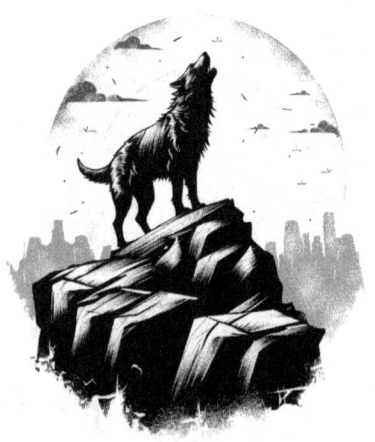

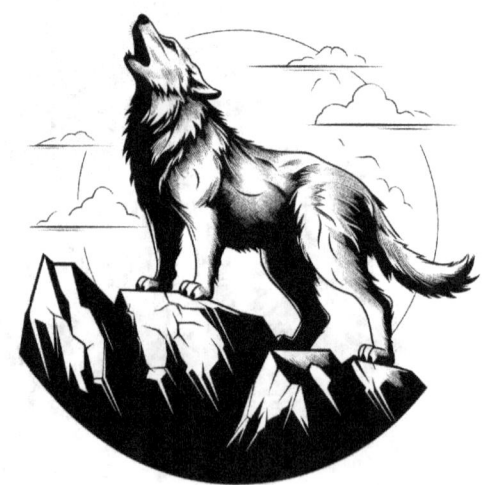

Lone wolf standing on a rocky cliff, howling at the moon, symbolizing independence, resilience, and the untamed spirit within.

The Wild Frontier

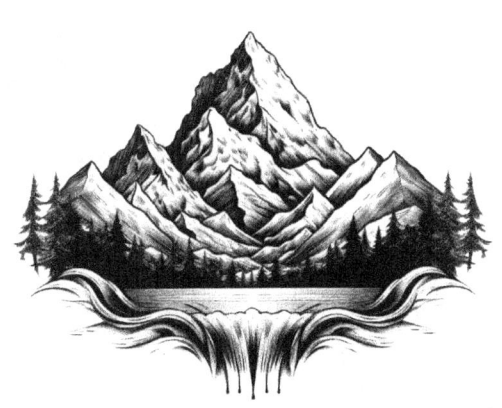

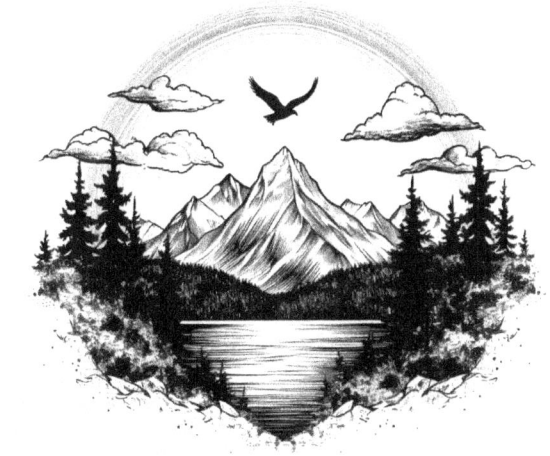

Majestic mountain range, with a roaring waterfall cascading down into a serene lake, symbolizing the awe-inspiring beauty and tranquility of nature.

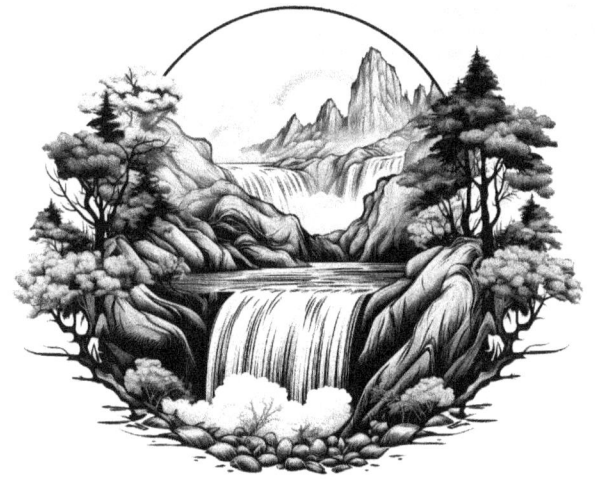

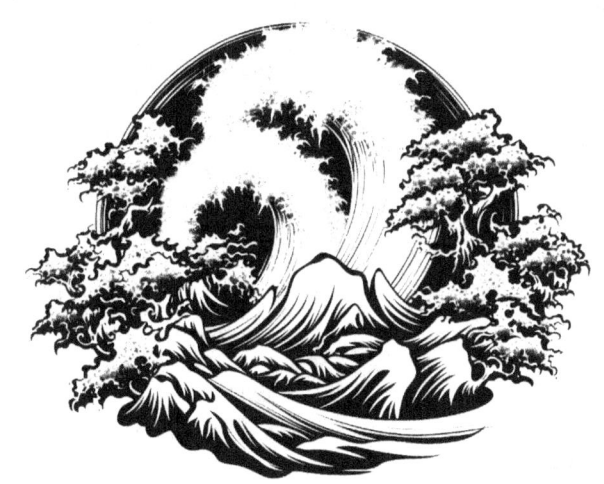

Raging waterfall surrounded by rocks and lush vegetation, representing the power, energy, and ever-flowing nature of life.

The Wild Frontier

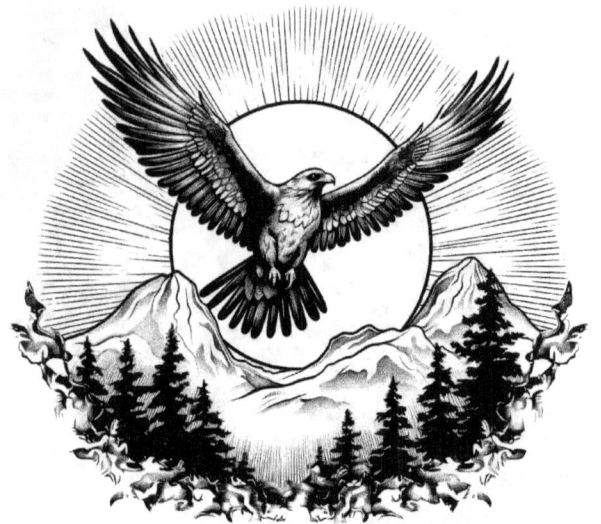

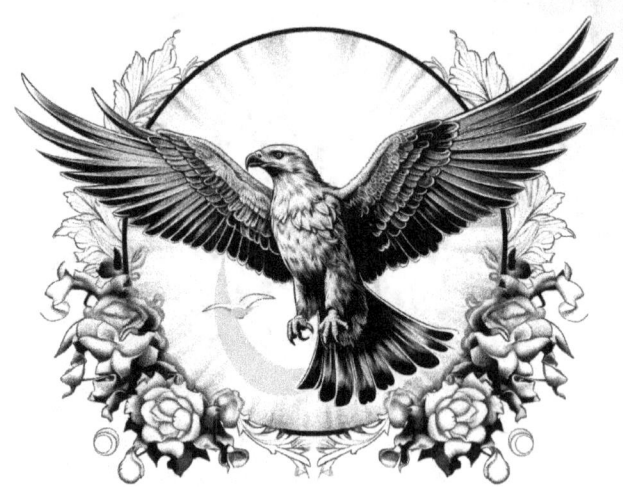

Soaring falcon against a backdrop of a setting sun, symbolizing freedom, vision, and the ability to rise above adversity with grace and strength.

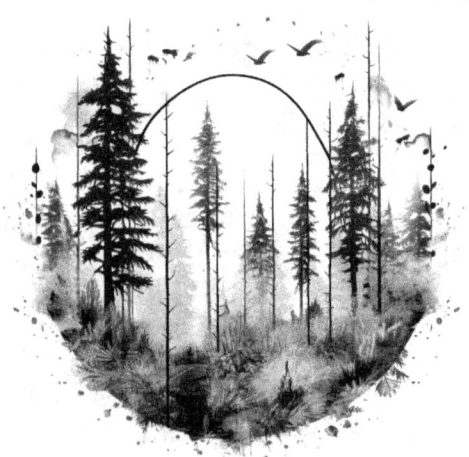

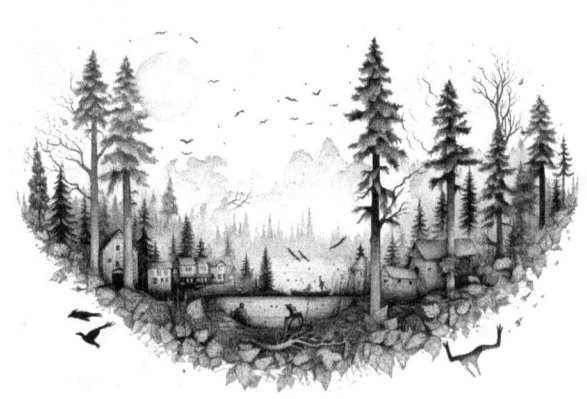

Detailed forest scene, with towering trees, dappled sunlight, and hidden wildlife, capturing the sense of adventure and the connection to the wilderness.

The Wild Frontier

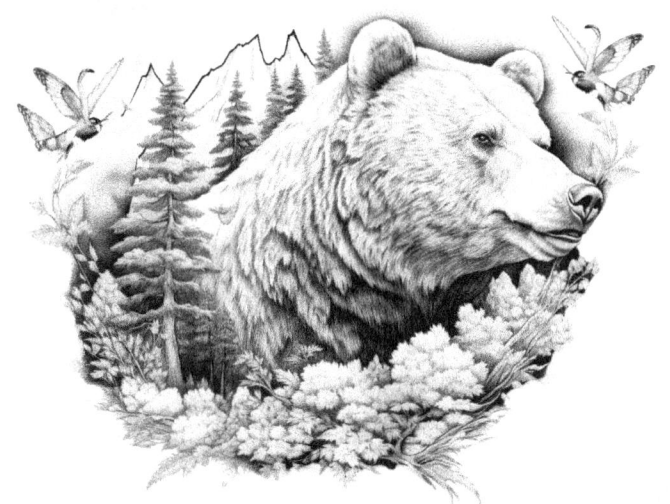

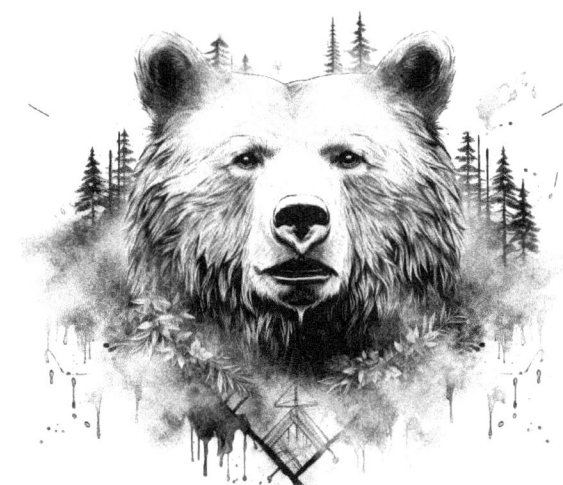

Detailed wildlife scene, with a bear, representing strength, grace, and the interconnectedness of all living beings.

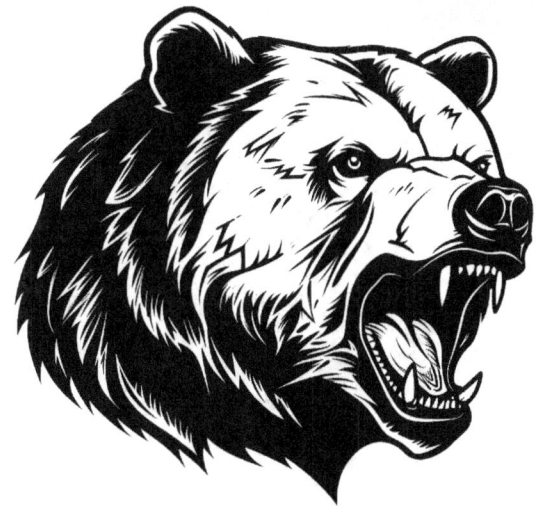

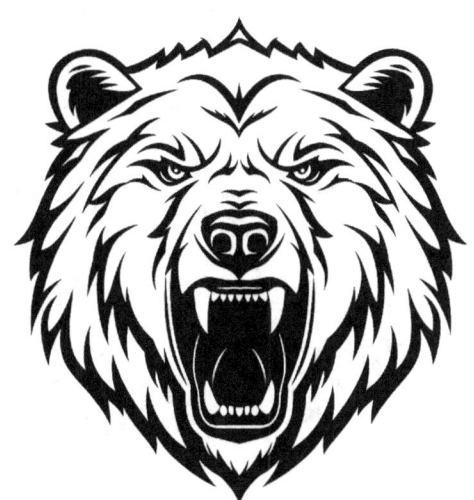

Fierce bear, with its piercing gaze and strong stance, representing strength, protection, and a primal connection to the wild.

The Wild Frontier

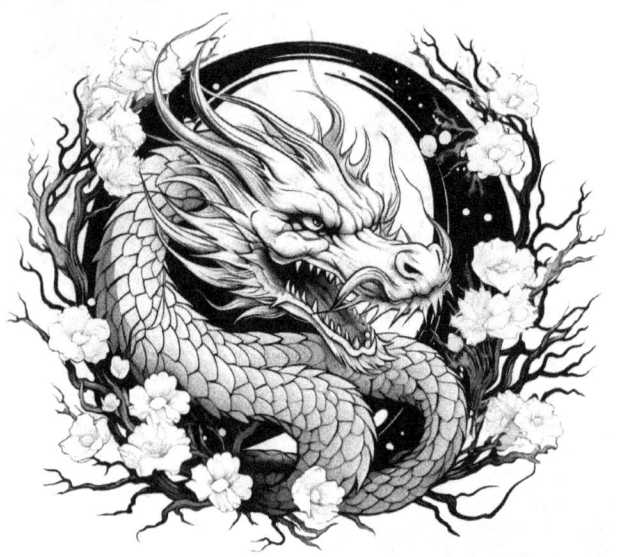

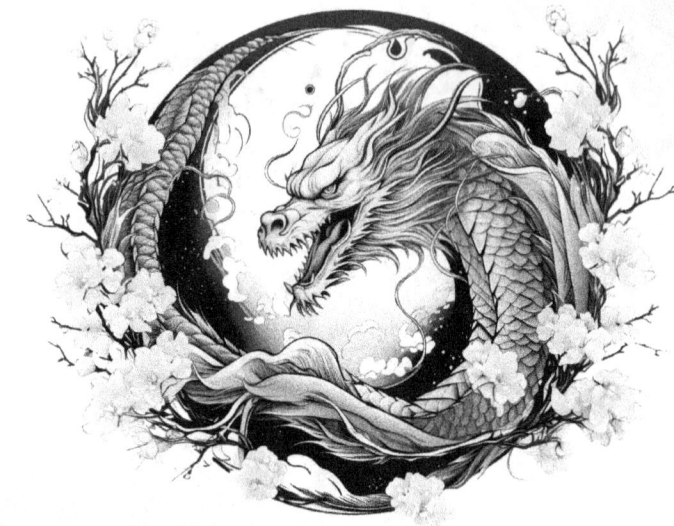

Fierce dragon intertwined with cherry blossoms, blending Eastern and Western symbolism, representing strength, rebirth, and the balance of yin and yang.

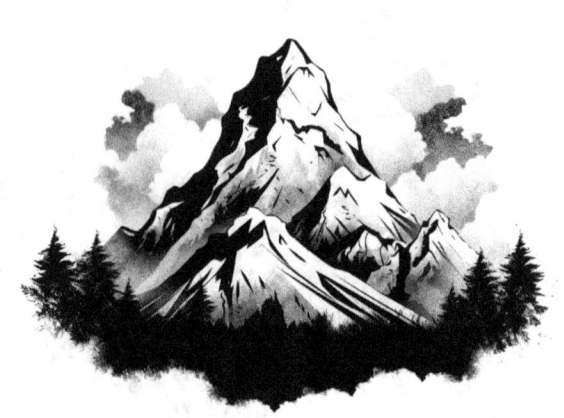

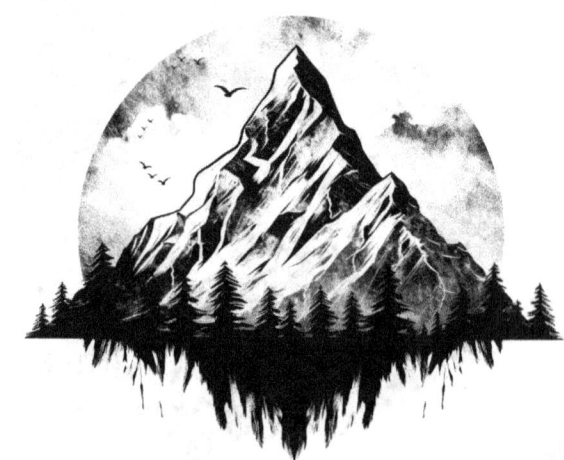

Silhouette of a mountain range, representing the challenges and victories that come with overcoming obstacles.

The Wild Frontier

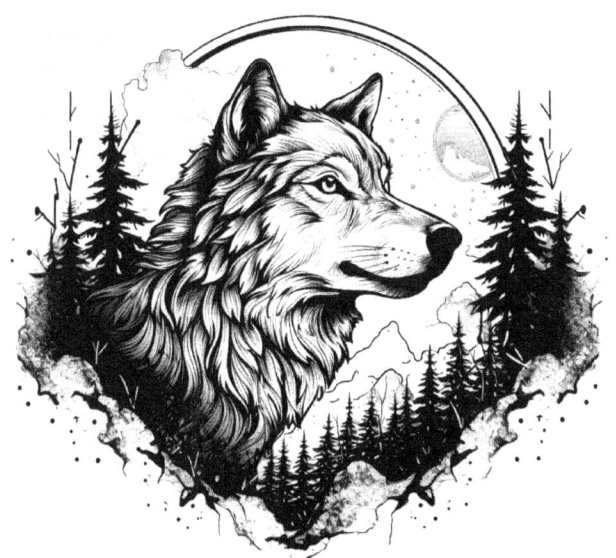

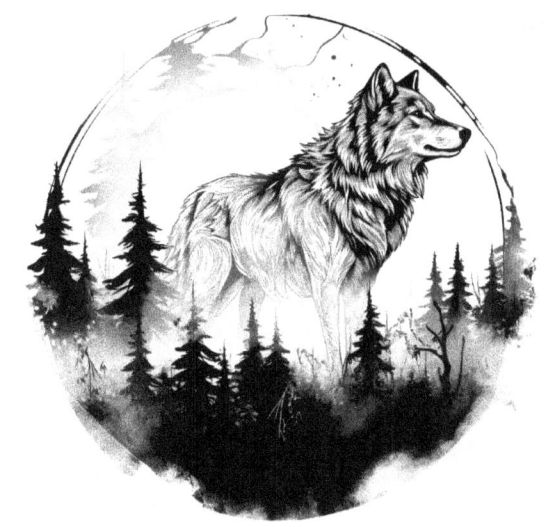

Wolf in a moonlit forest,
embodying loyalty, intuition, and
the untamed spirit of the wild.

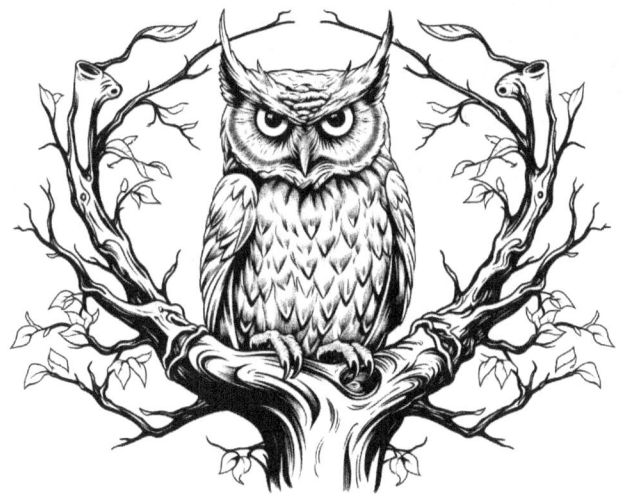

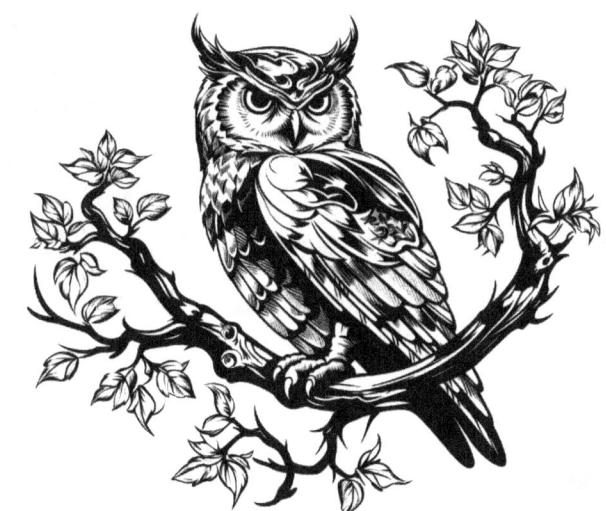

Owl perched on a tree branch,
symbolizing wisdom, intuition, and
the nocturnal beauty of the
wilderness.

The Wild Frontier

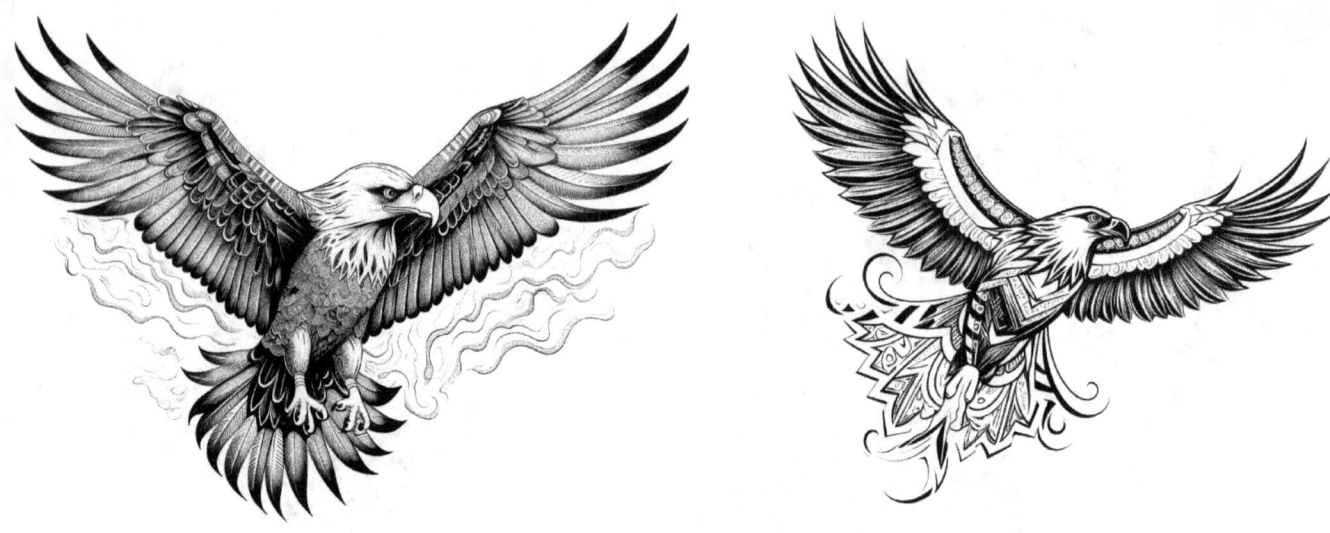

Eagle in flight, symbolizing freedom, vision, and a connection to the limitless skies.

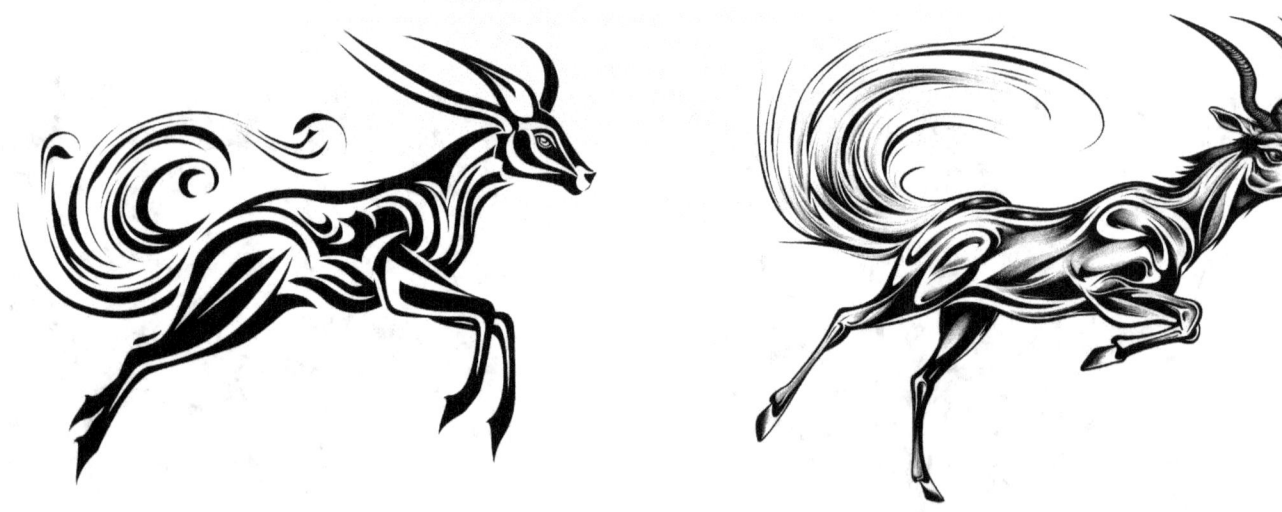

Grace and power of a leaping gazelle, symbolizing swiftness, agility, and a connection to the African savannah.

The Wild Frontier

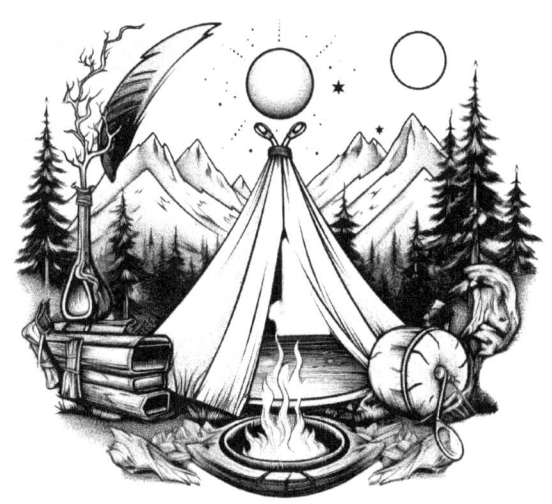

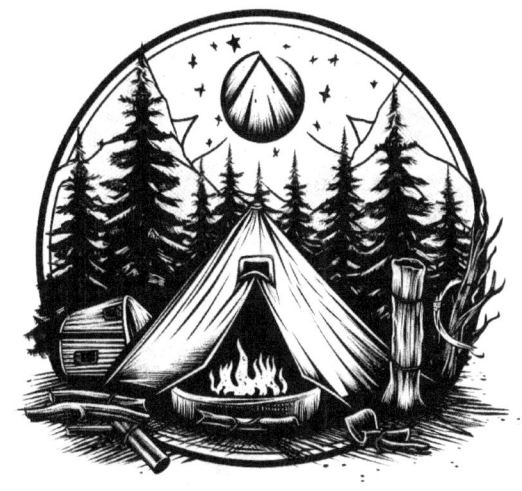

Campfire with a tent and camping gear, evoking memories of outdoor adventures, camaraderie, and the simple joys of nature.

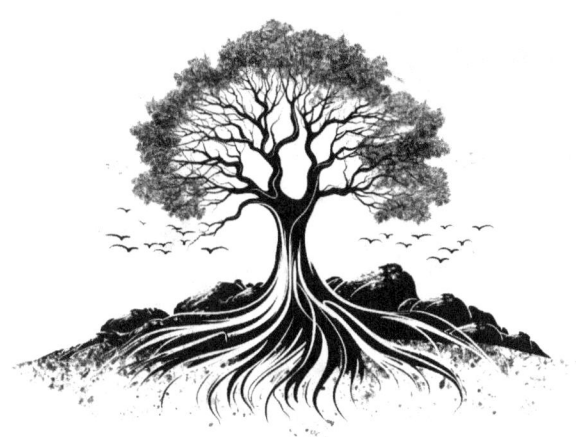

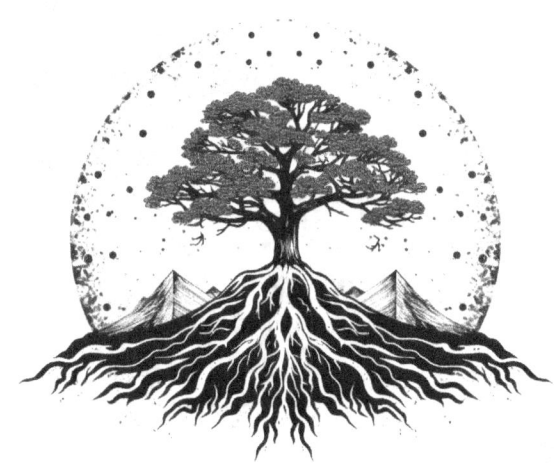

Lone tree on a hill, with roots extending deep into the ground, symbolizing grounding, growth, and resilience.

The Wild Frontier

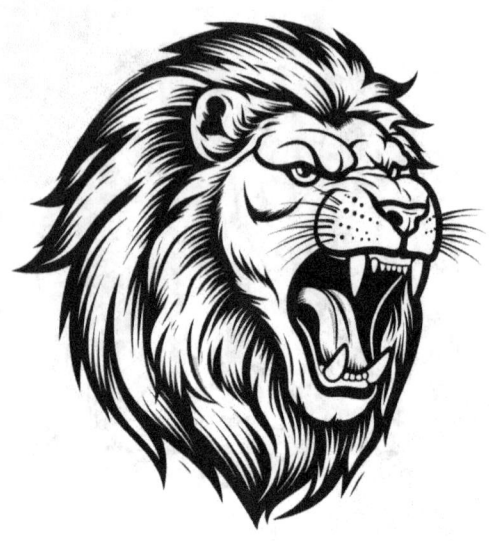 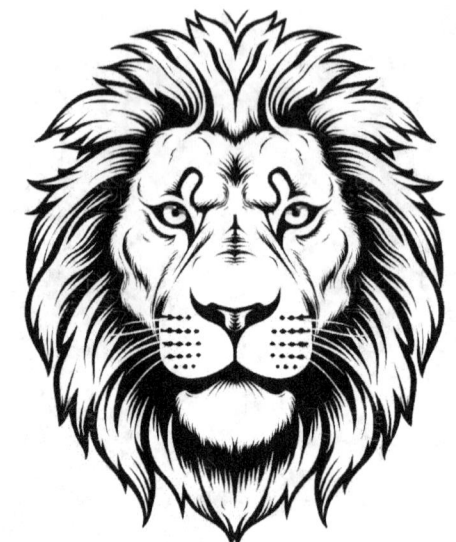

Roaring lion, in the savannah, symbolizing courage, leadership, and a primal connection to the wild.

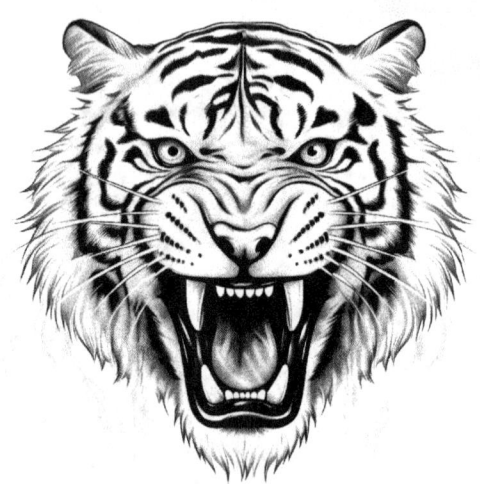 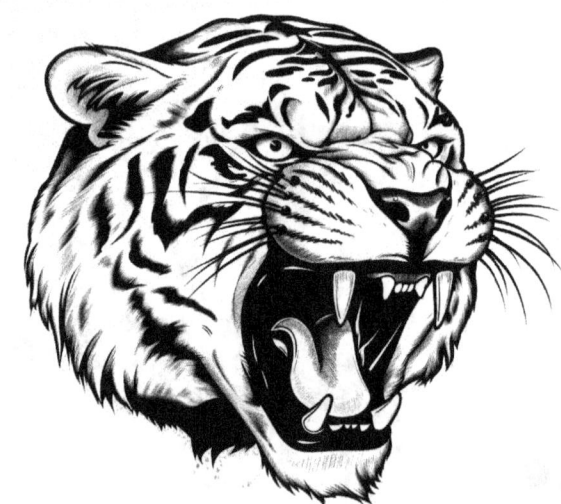

Roaring tiger, representing strength, power, and the untamed spirit within.

The Wild Frontier

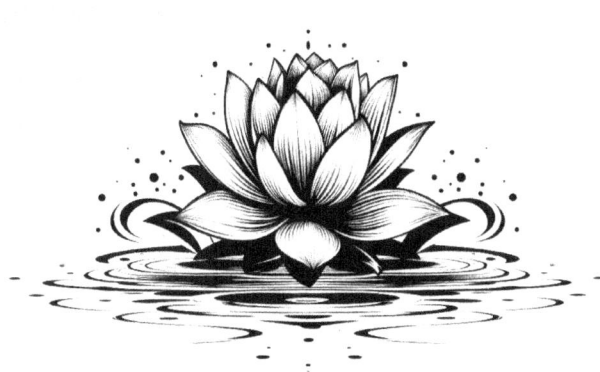

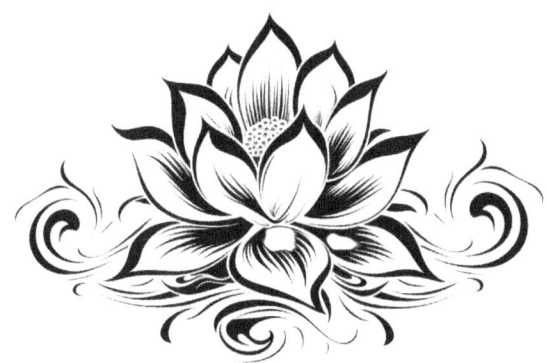

Lotus flower rising from muddy waters, symbolizing purity, enlightenment, and the ability to find inner peace amidst life's challenges.

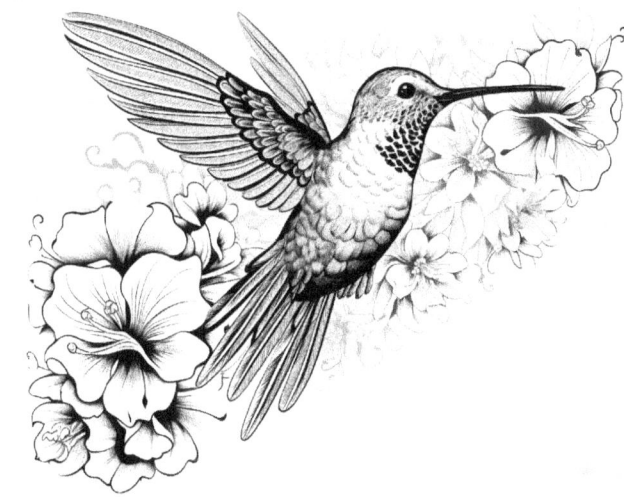

Vibrant hummingbird amidst a tapestry of tropical flowers, representing joy, resilience, and the delicate balance of nature.

Modern Masculinity

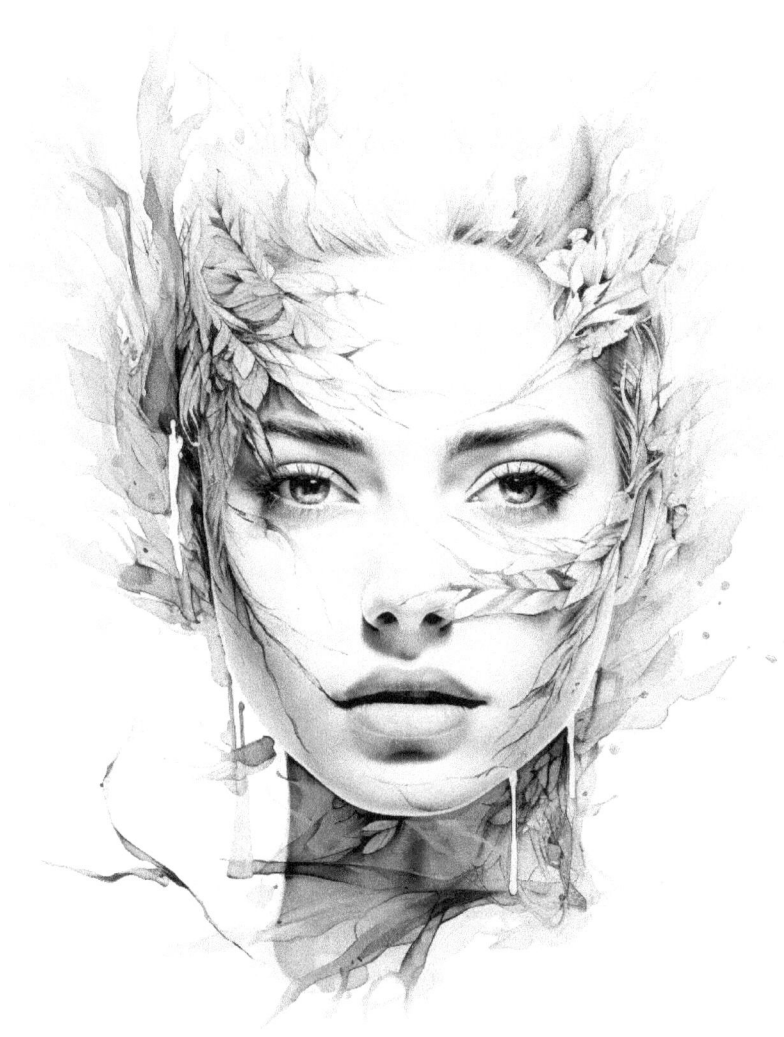

Modern Masculinity
Redefining Contemporary Ink

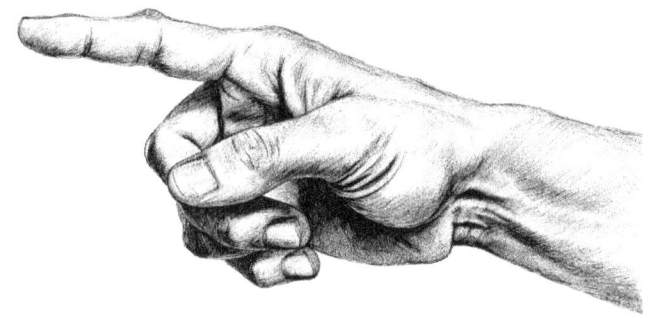 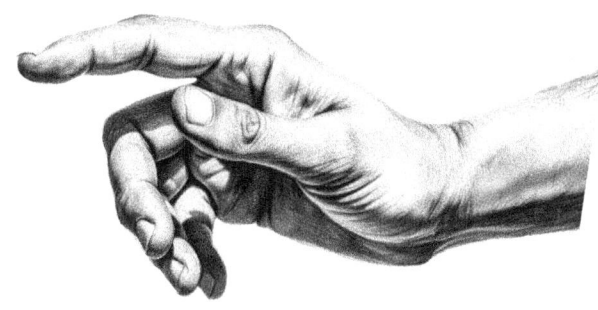

Detailed pencil sketch of a human hand, symbolizing the artist's touch, craftsmanship, and the ability to bring life to the blank canvas.

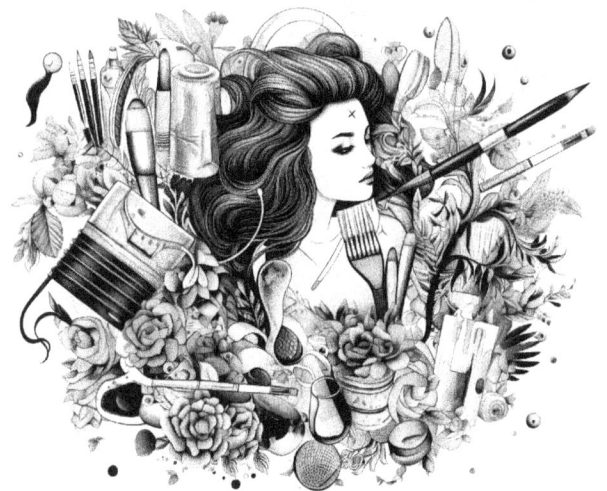 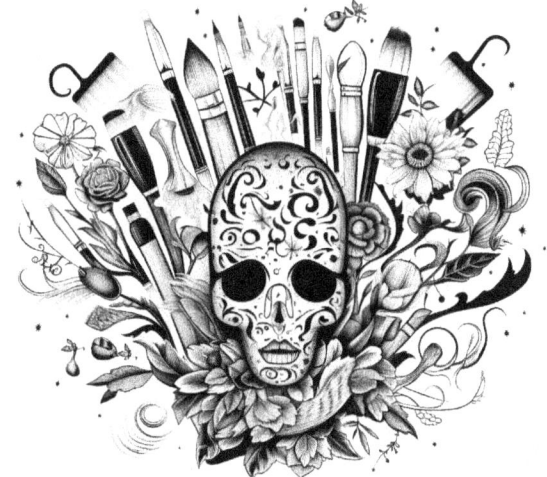

Artistic tools like paintbrushes and pencils, representing the multifaceted nature of creativity and the endless possibilities of artistic exploration.

Modern Masculinity

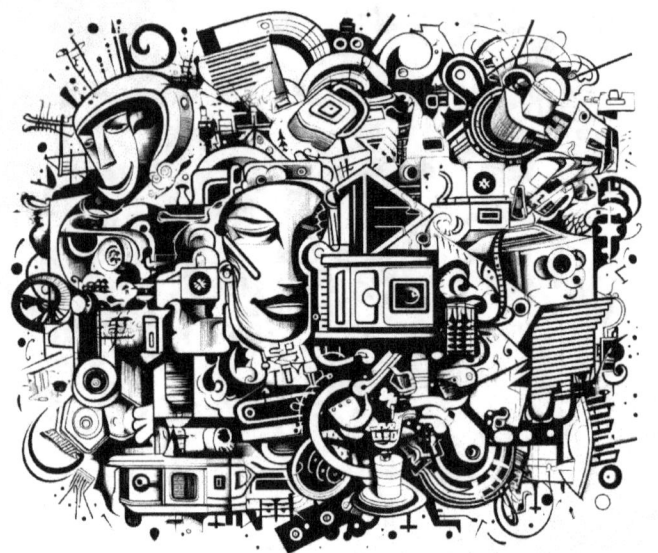
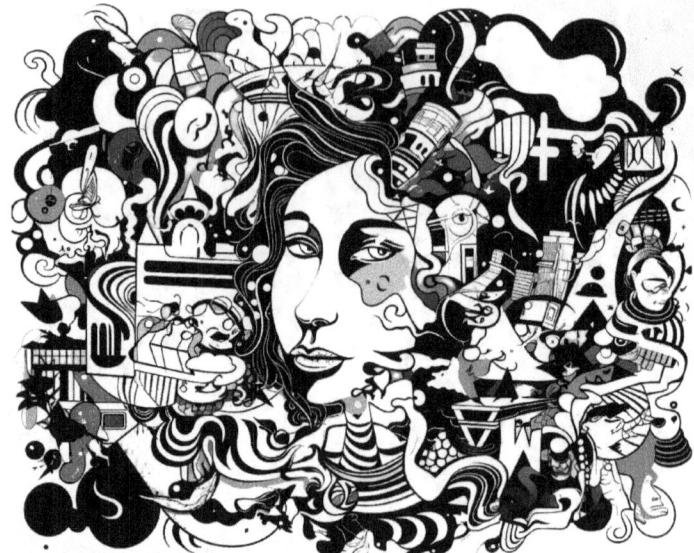

Graffiti-style mural, incorporating various elements like street art, symbols, and abstract shapes, symbolizing the rebellious spirit of artistic expression.

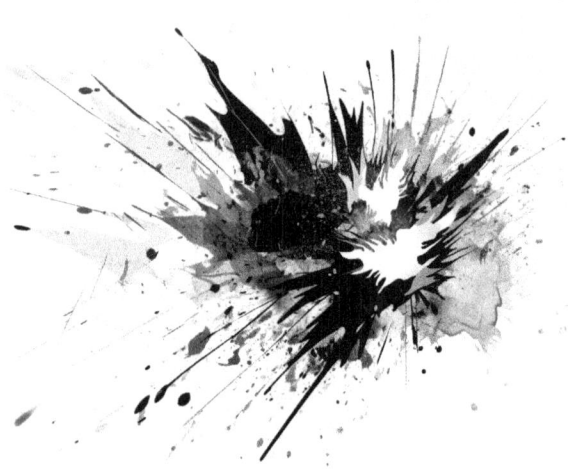
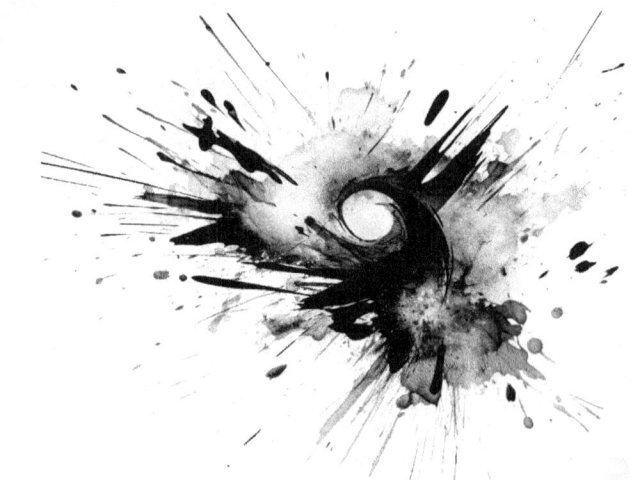

Contemporary abstract artwork, with bold brushstrokes, splatters, and a mix of textures, reflecting the freedom, experimentation, and innovation of modern art.

Modern Masculinity

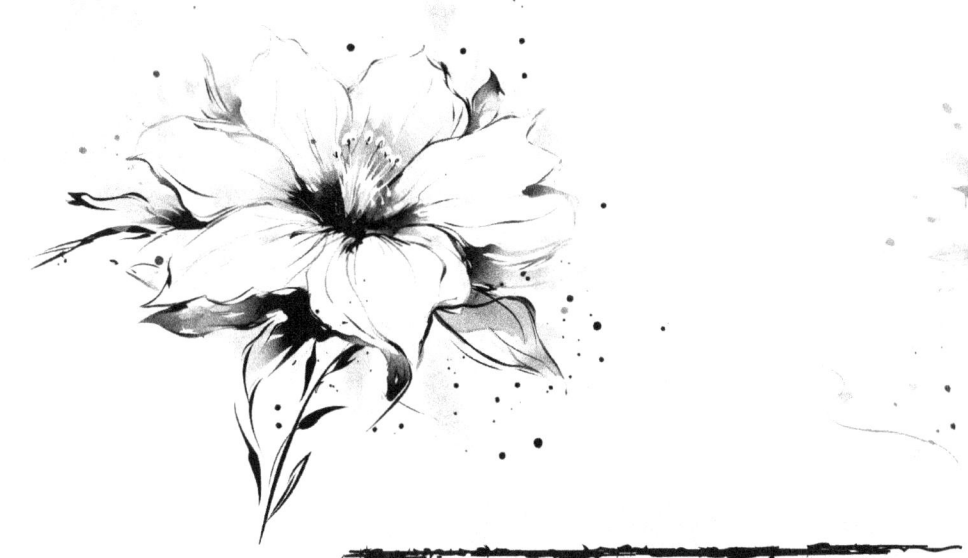

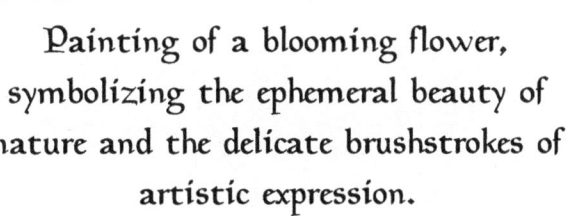

Painting of a blooming flower, symbolizing the ephemeral beauty of nature and the delicate brushstrokes of artistic expression.

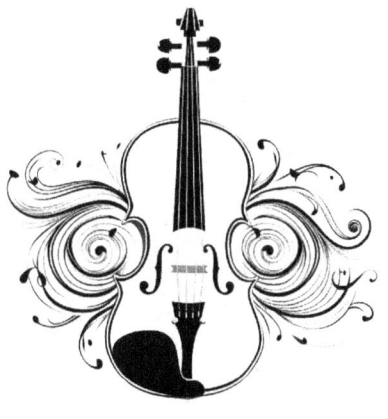
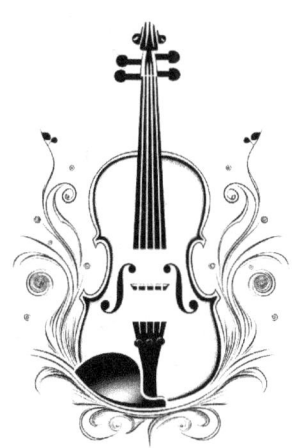

Minimalist outline of a violin, symbolizing the harmonious combination of music and visual art and the ability of both to convey emotions.

Modern Masculinity

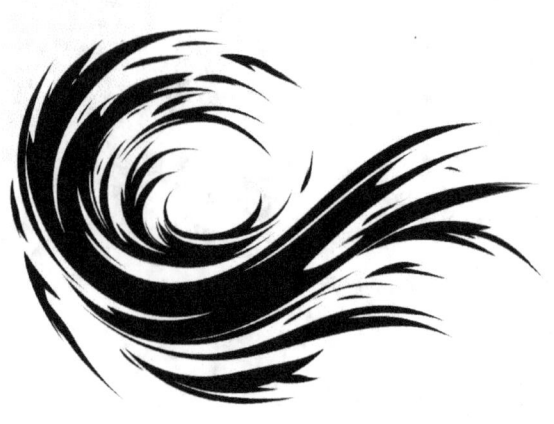 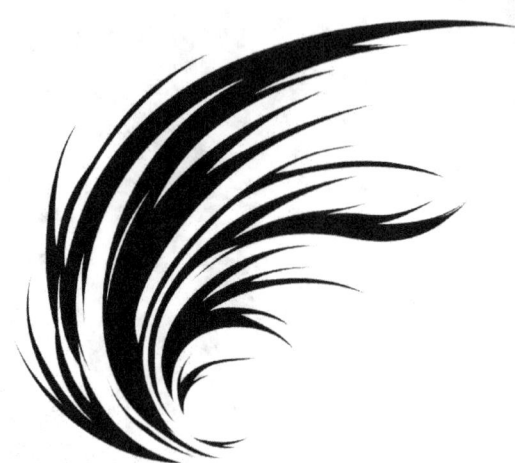

Stylized brushstroke, symbolizing the power of artistic expression and the ability to create beauty from simple gestures.

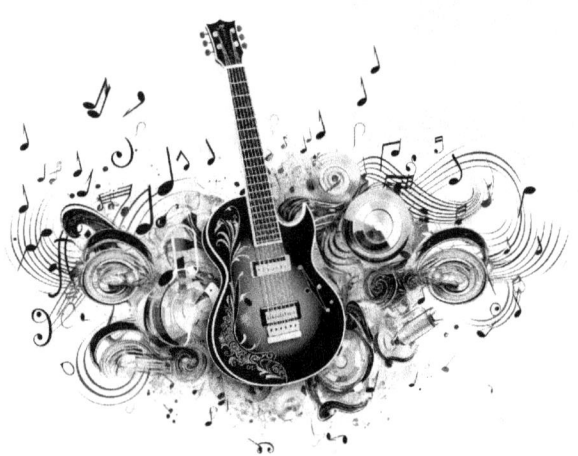 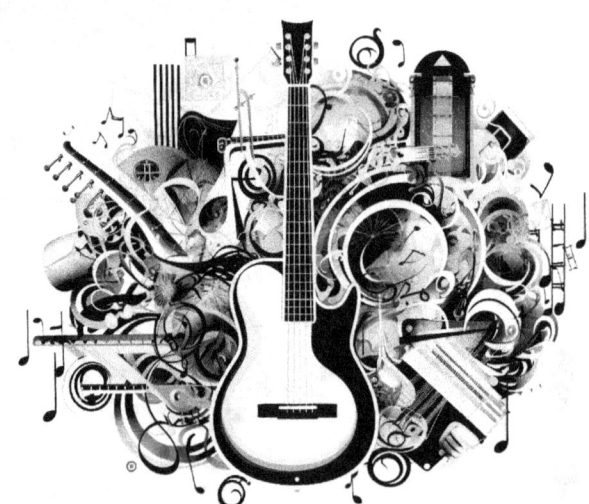

Composition of musical notes, instruments, and soundwaves, representing the synergy between music and art and the ability of both to evoke emotions and transcend boundaries.

Modern Masculinity

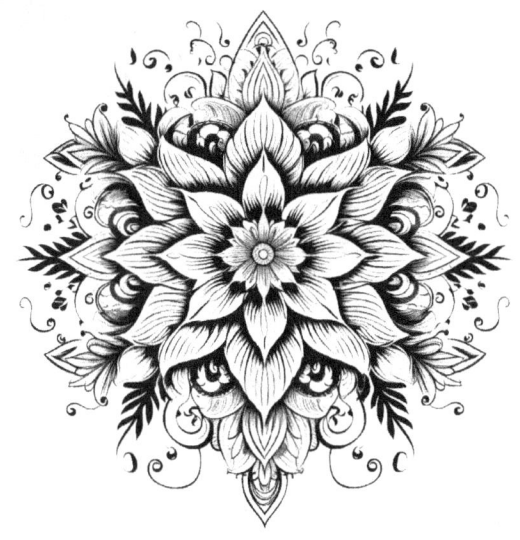

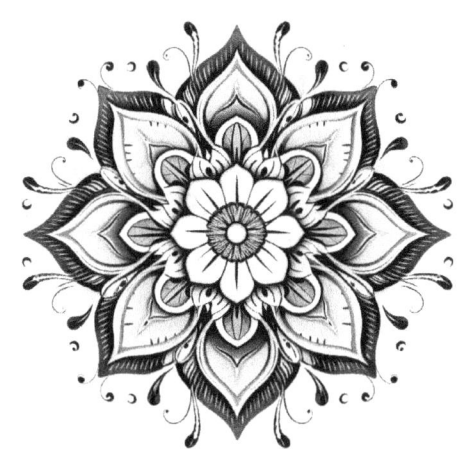

Mandala design, with intricate patterns and symmetrical geometry, symbolizing balance, spiritual growth, and the harmony of artistic creation.

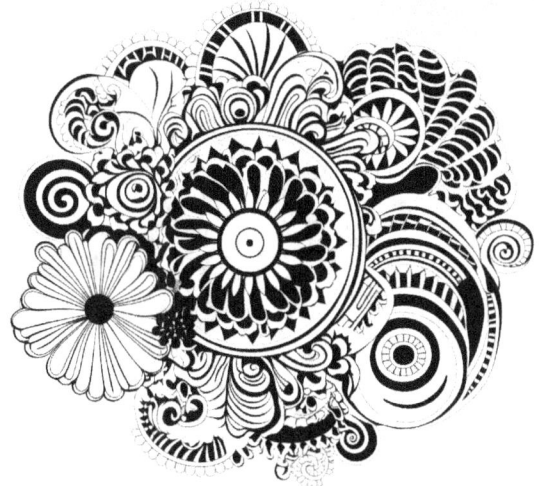

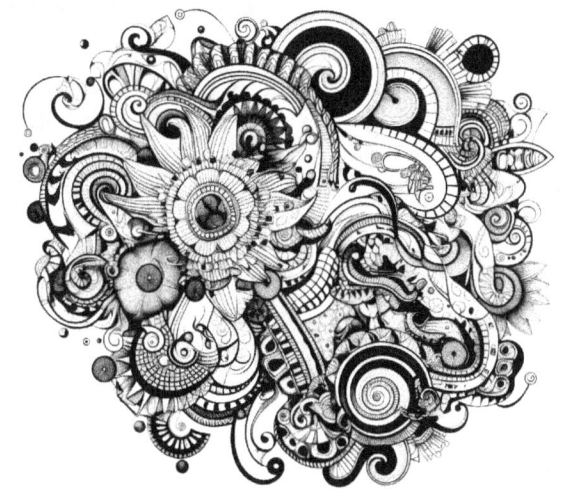

Mosaic pattern, with intricate tile work, symbolizing the beauty of diverse cultures and the art of bringing together fragments to create a unified whole.

Modern Masculinity

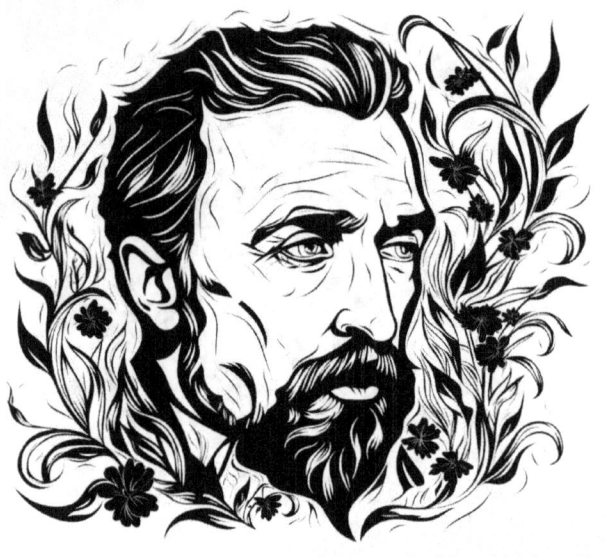 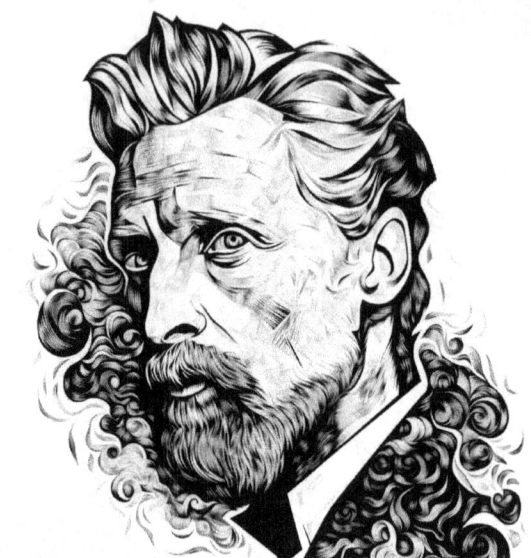

Portrait of Vincent van Gogh, capturing his iconic self-portrait, paying homage to his artistic genius and his enduring impact on the art world.

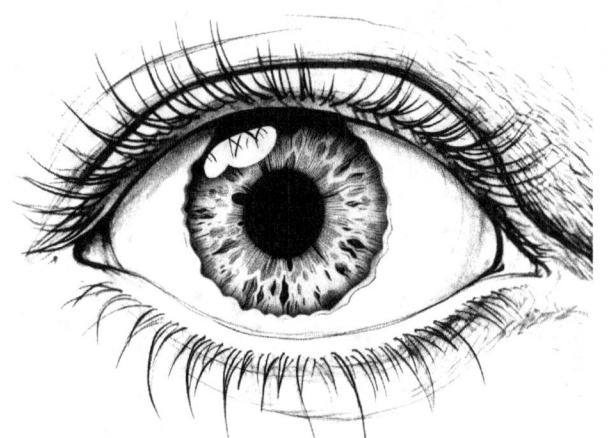 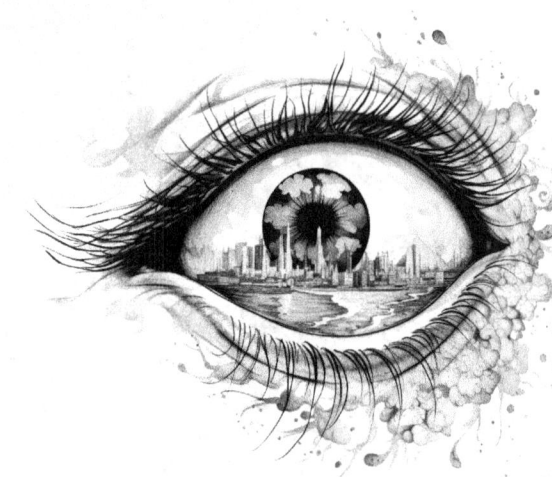

Sketch of a human eye, symbolizing the power of observation, perception, and the exploration of the inner self through art.

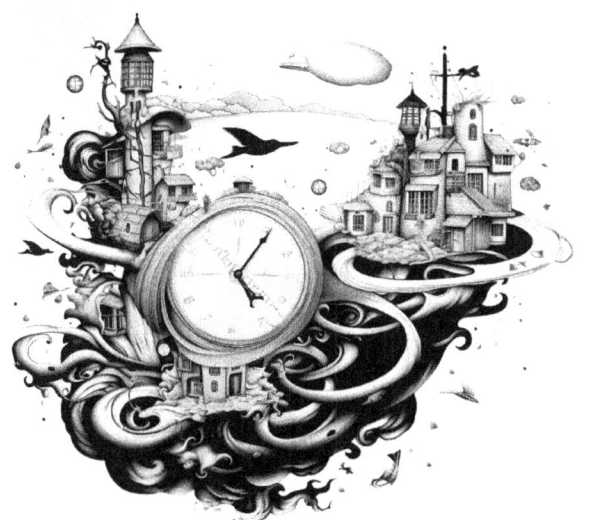

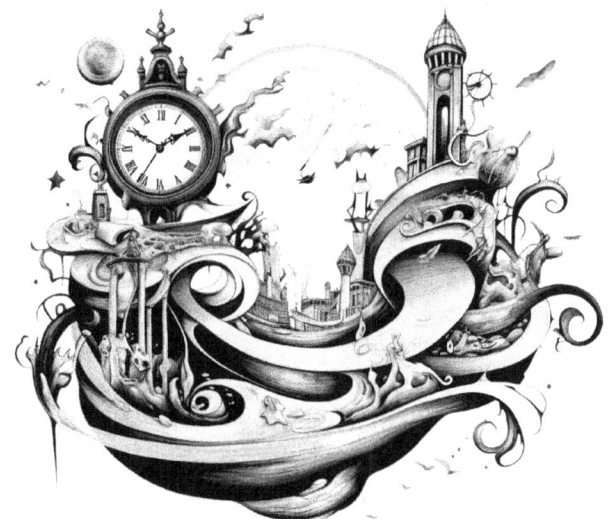

Surrealistic landscape with melting clocks, flying fish, and floating objects, capturing the spirit of Salvador Dali's artistic vision and the concept of bending reality.

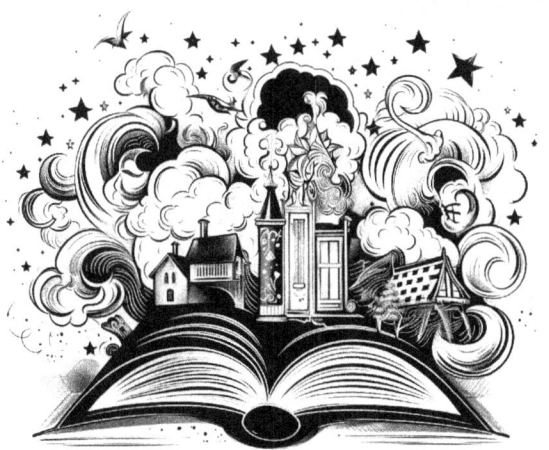

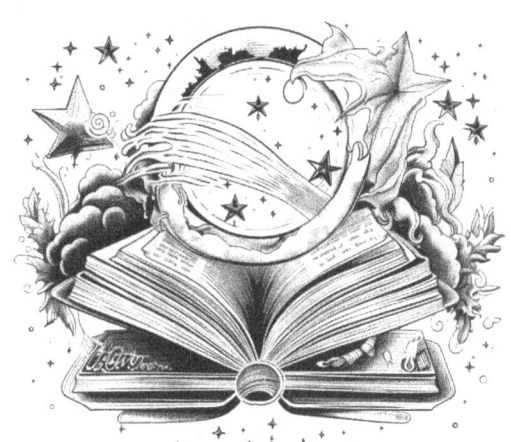

Whimsical illustration of a book open to a magical world, representing the power of storytelling and the imaginative realms that art can create.

Modern Masculinity

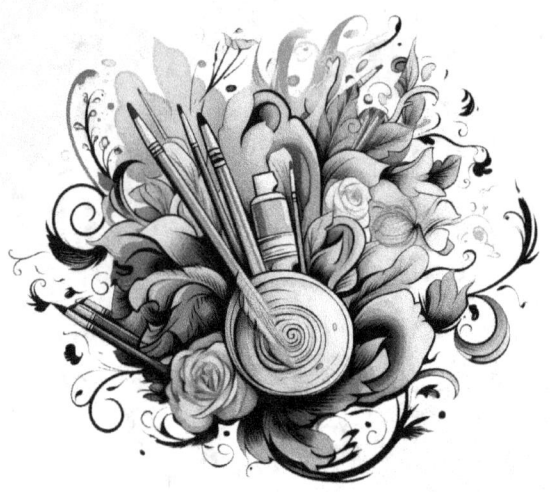

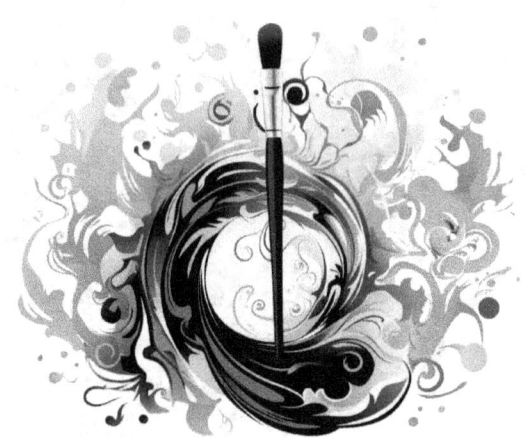

Classic art palette with paintbrushes and a spectrum of colors, representing the artist's toolkit and the boundless possibilities of artistic creation.

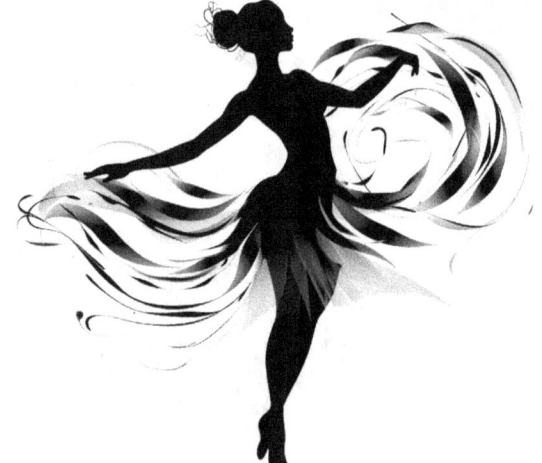

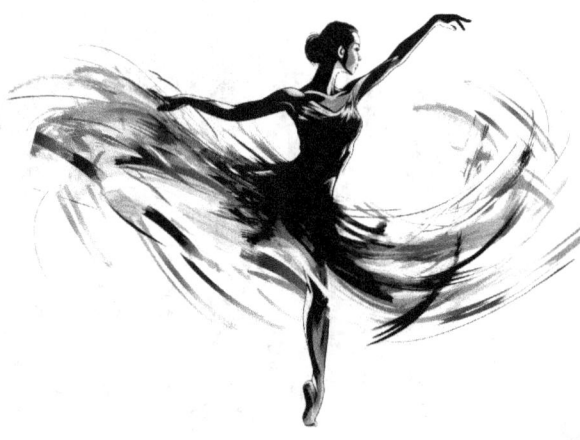

Drawing of a dancer in mid-motion, capturing the grace, fluidity, and rhythm of dance as a form of artistic expression.

Modern Masculinity

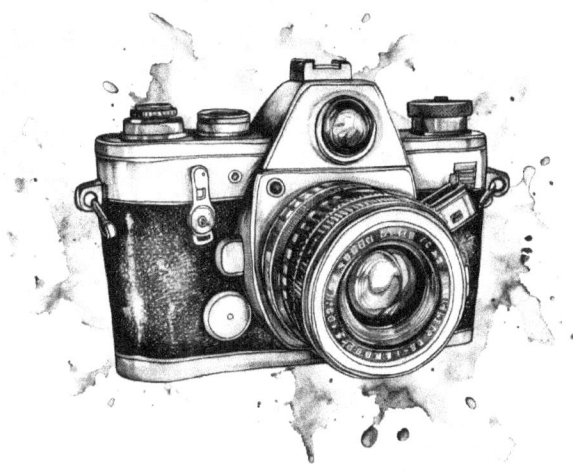

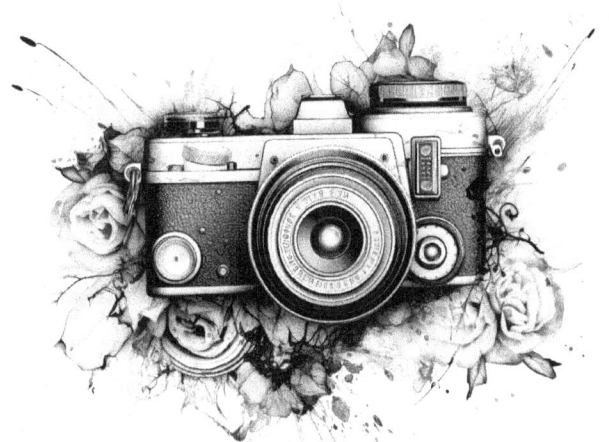

Black-and-white camera, capturing the essence of photography as a form of artistic expression and the ability to freeze moments in time.

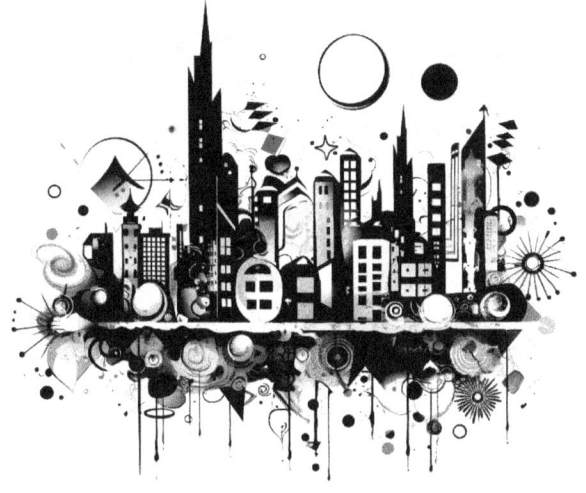

Vibrant and abstract interpretation of a city skyline at night, incorporating bold geometric shapes, and dynamic lines to evoke a sense of urban energy and creativity.

Modern Masculinity

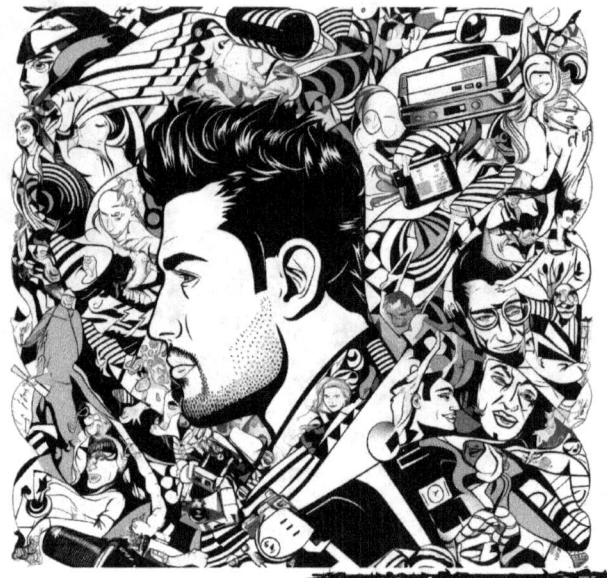

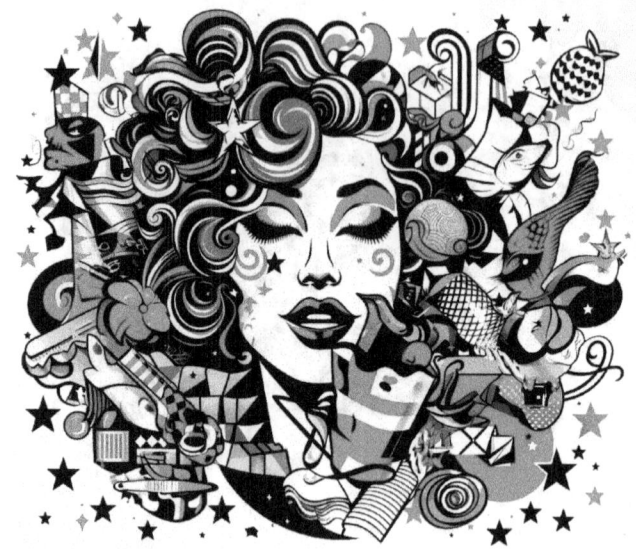

Vivid pop art—inspired design, comic book—style elements, and iconic imagery, celebrating the vibrancy of popular culture and its influence on art.

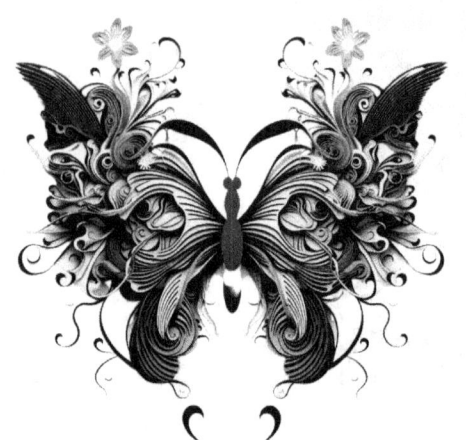

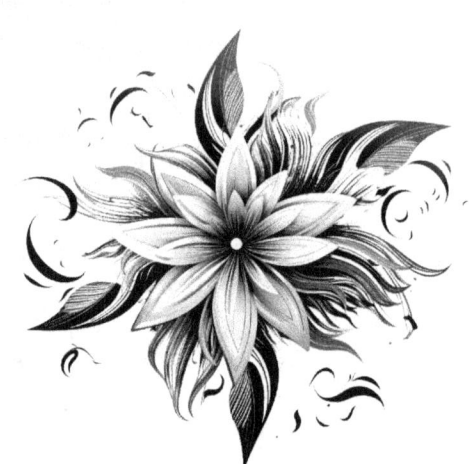

Origami design, symbolizing the art of folding paper and the meticulous nature of artistic craftsmanship.

The Spirit Within

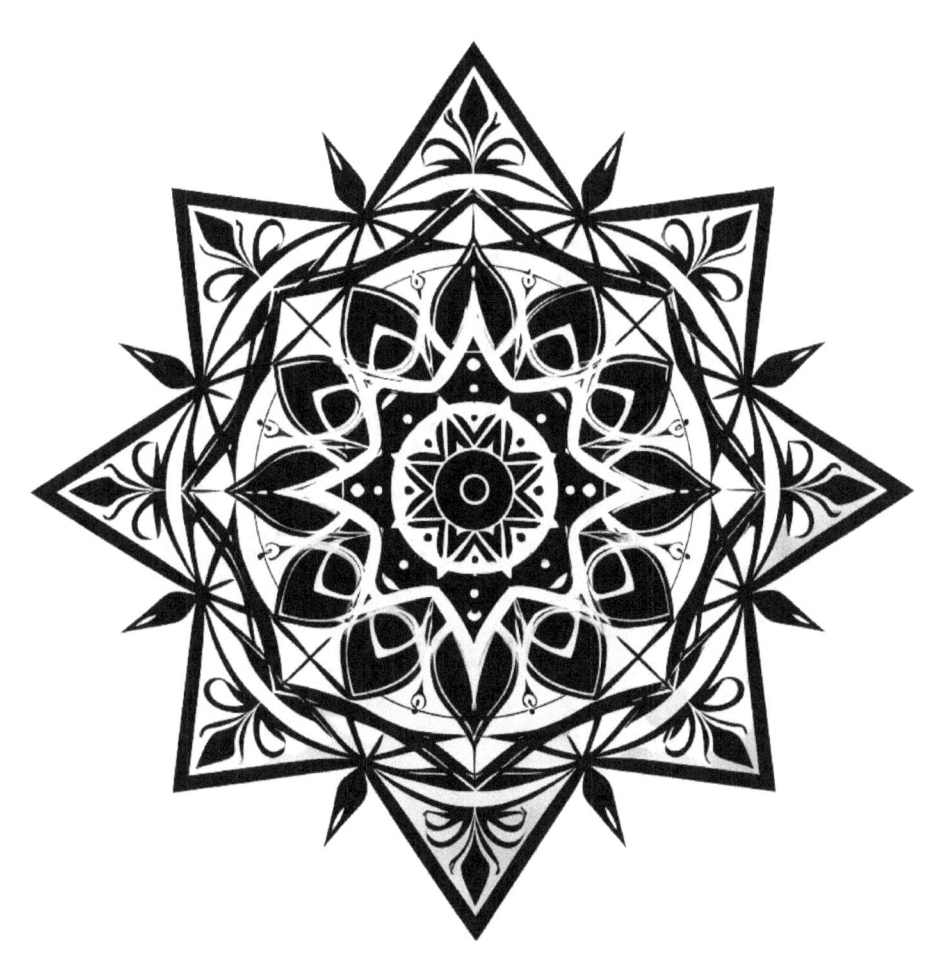

The Spirit Within
Illuminating the Inner Self

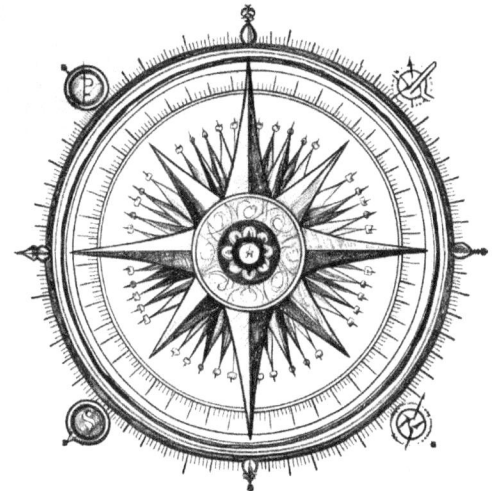

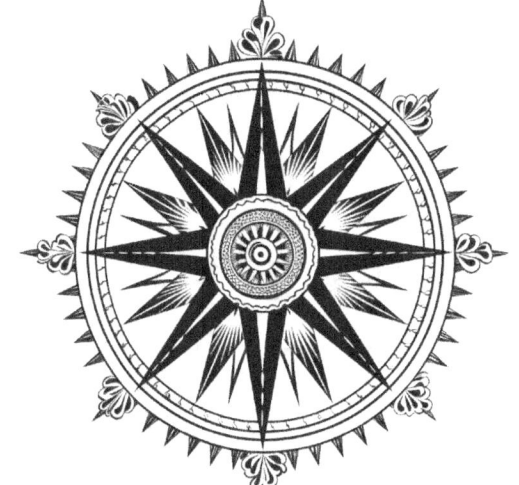

Compass rose symbolizing the journey of finding one's true calling and living with intention.

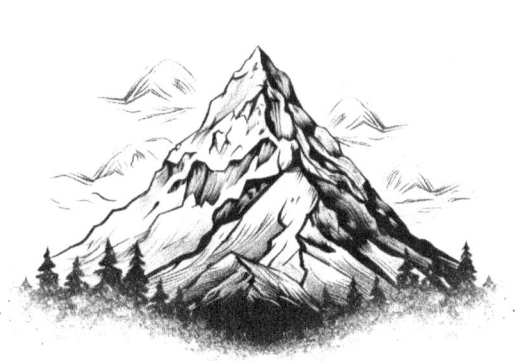

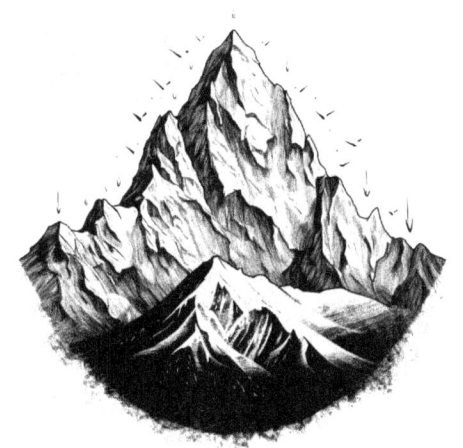

Detailed mountain range, representing the determination, perseverance, and the pursuit of conquering personal goals and reaching new heights.

The Spirit Within

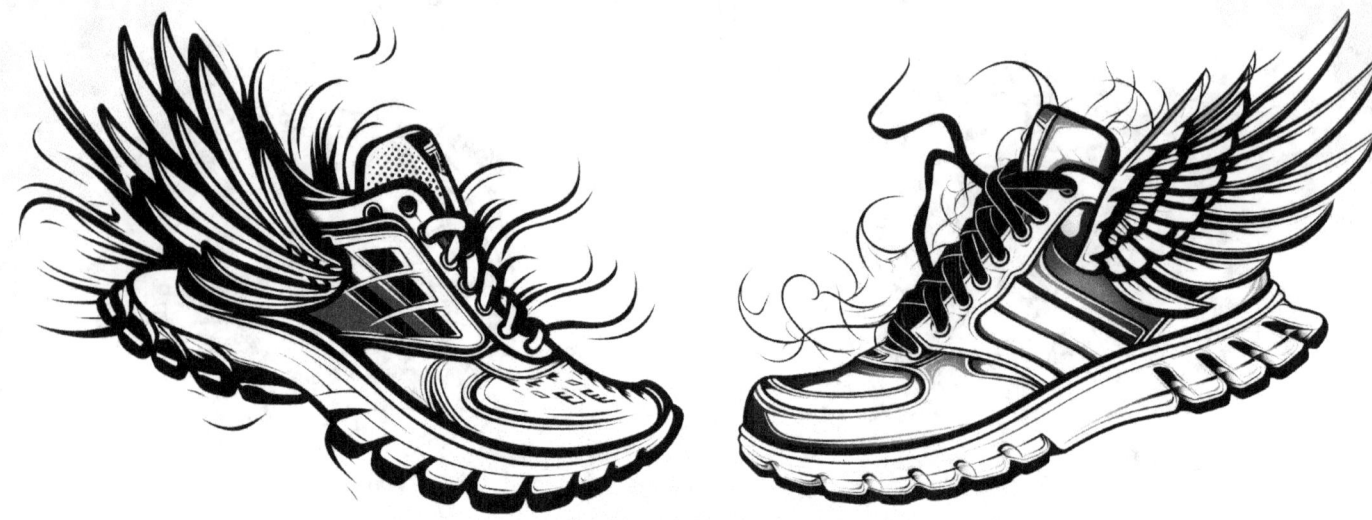

Running shoe with wings, representing the pursuit of physical fitness and the exhilaration of pushing one's limits in sports or other physical activities.

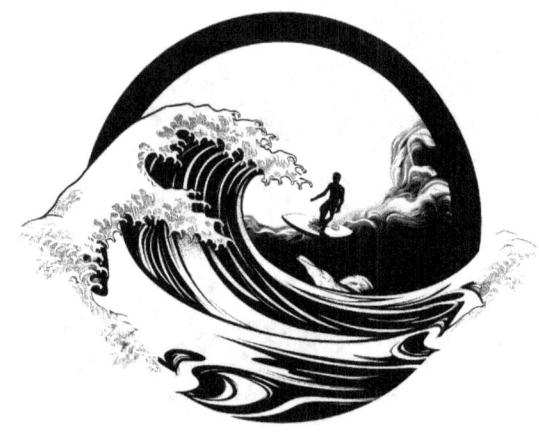
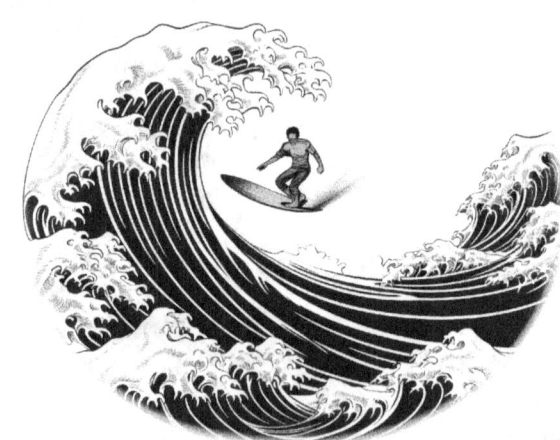

Serene ocean wave with a surfer riding it, symbolizing the love for surfing and the freedom and joy it brings in riding the waves.

The Spirit Within

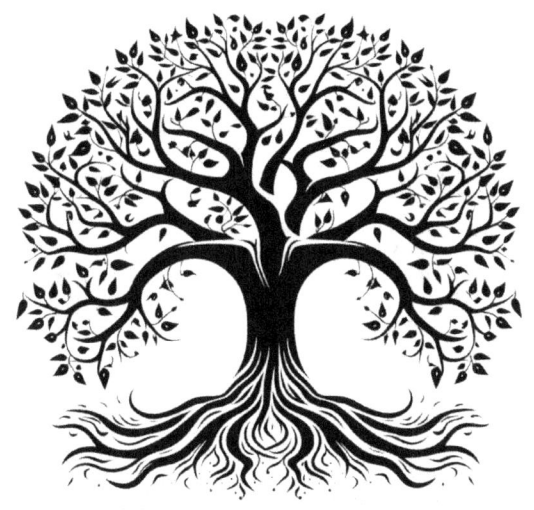

Tree with roots spreading into the ground and branches reaching towards the sky, symbolizing the interconnectedness of life, personal growth, and the pursuit of purpose.

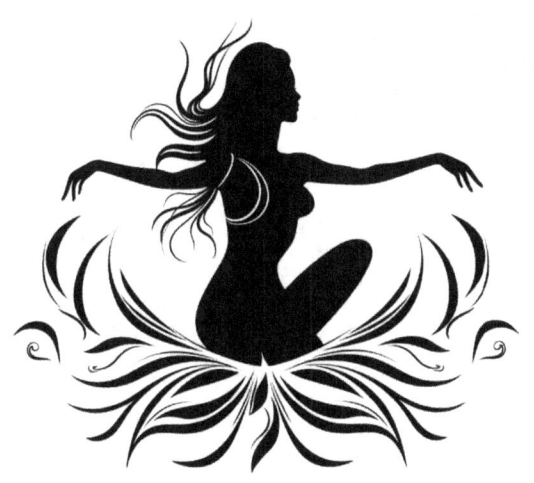

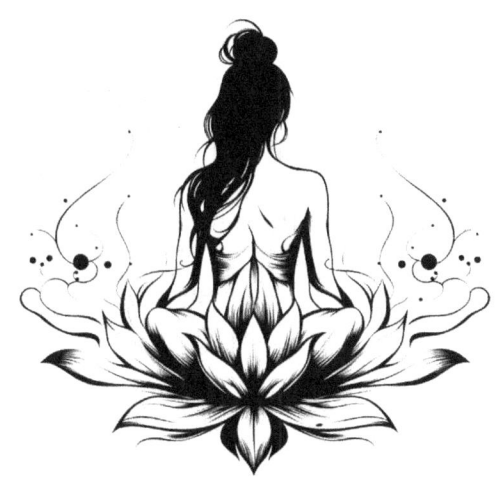

Yoga pose with a lotus flower, representing a passion for wellness, mindfulness, and the pursuit of inner balance and peace.

The Spirit Within

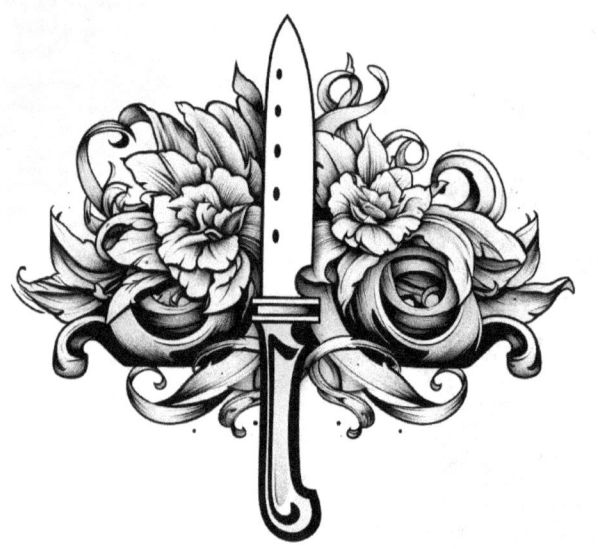

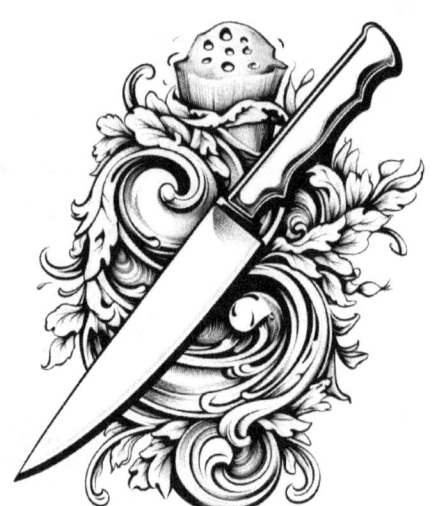

Chef's knife, representing a passion for culinary arts, cooking, and the creation of delicious meals.

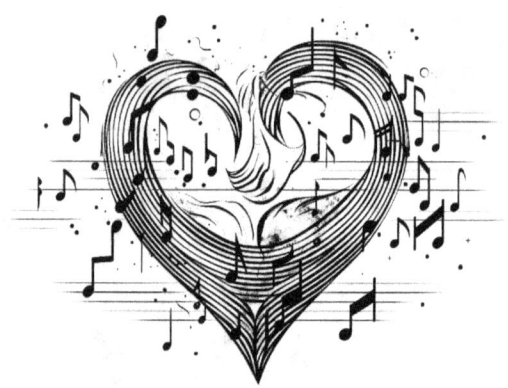

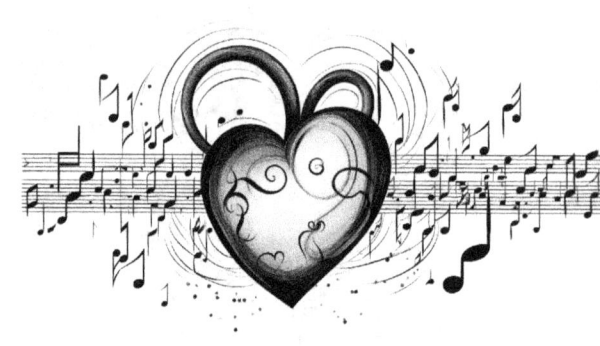

heart intertwined with musical notes, representing the passion and rhythm of music and the importance of following one's heart.

The Spirit Within

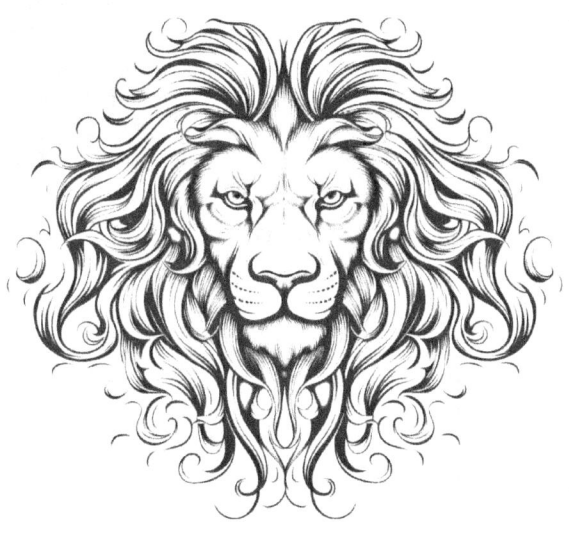

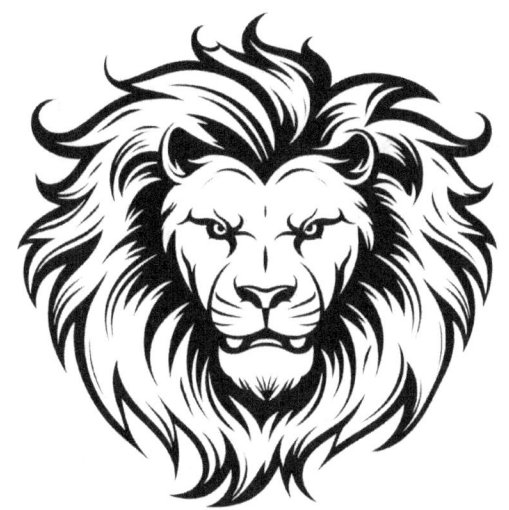

Lion's head, symbolizing courage, strength, and the fierce determination to chase one's dreams and passions.

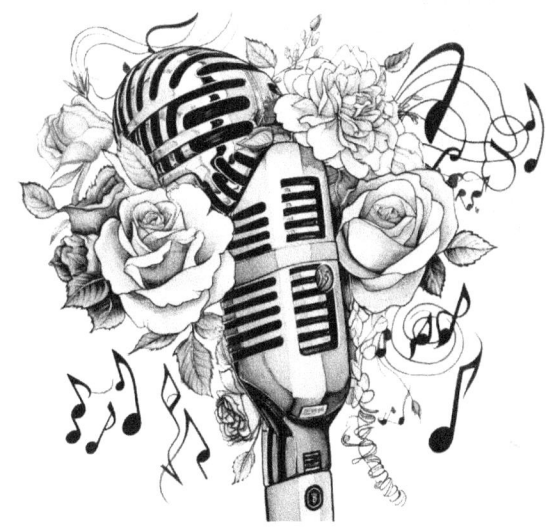

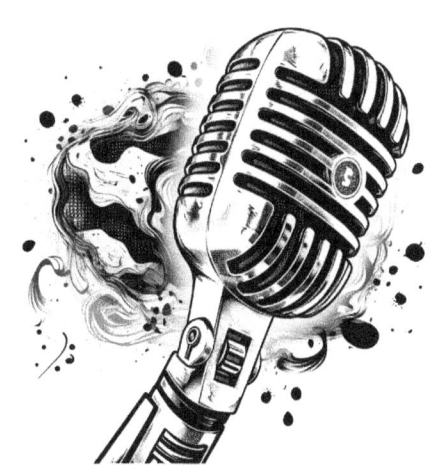

Microphone with musical notes, representing a passion for singing, performing, and the expression of one's voice.

The Spirit Within

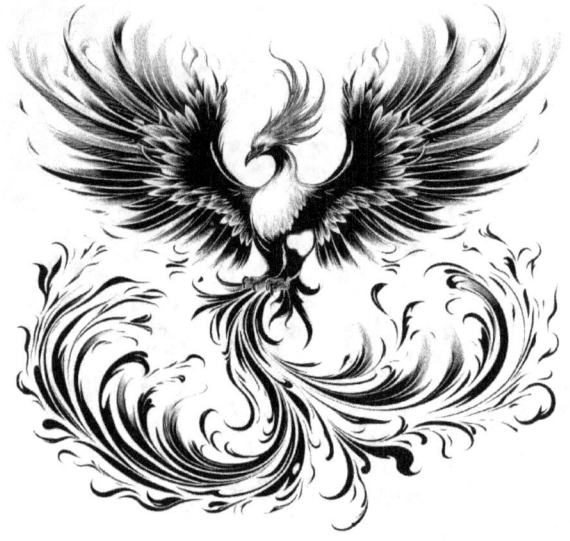

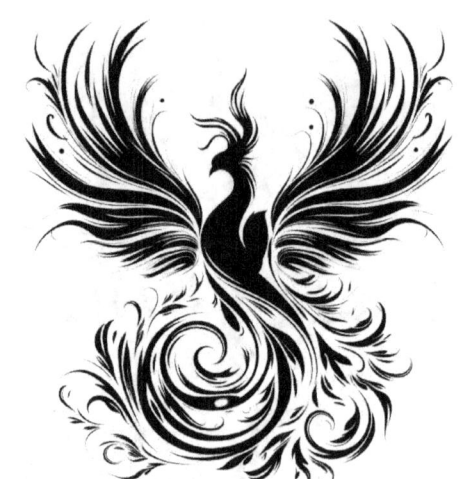

Phoenix rising from the ashes, symbolizing resilience, rebirth, and the transformative power of pursuing one's passion.

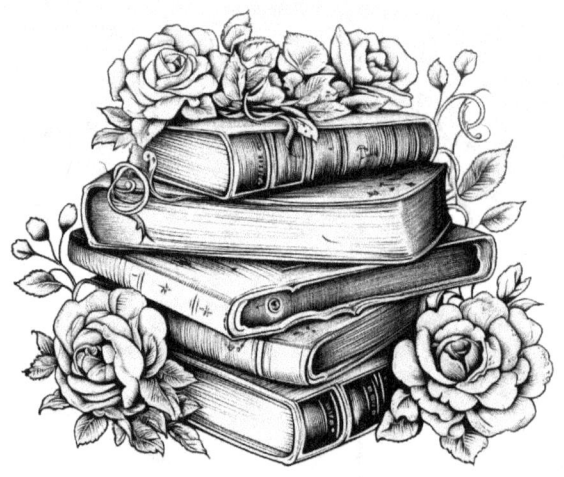

Stack of books with intricate designs on their spines, representing a love for literature, knowledge, and the pursuit of intellectual passions.

The Spirit Within

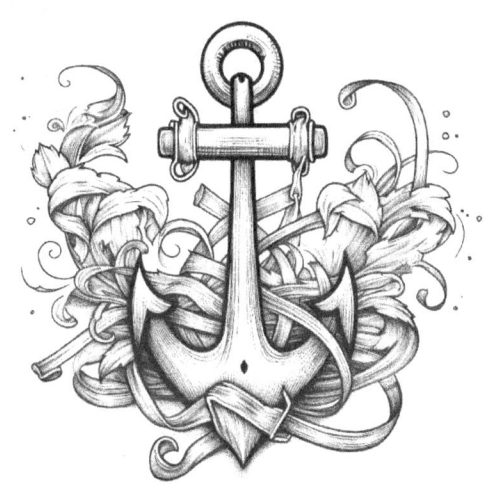

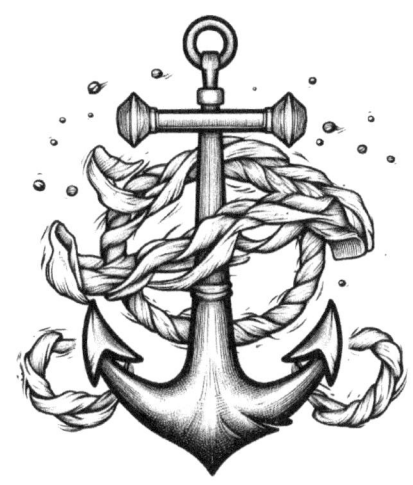

Anchor, symbolizing the balance between stability and creative expression, and the pursuit of writing or other artistic endeavors.

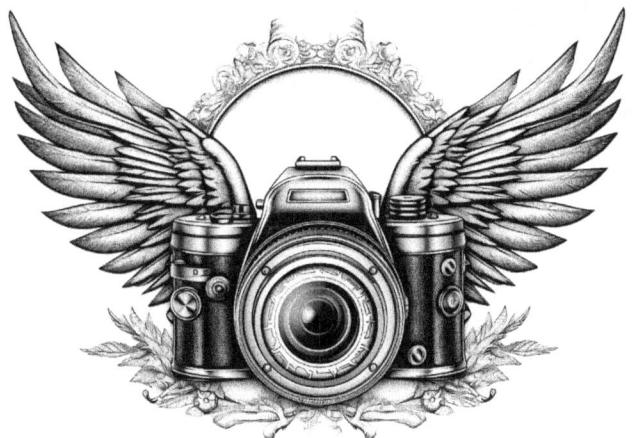

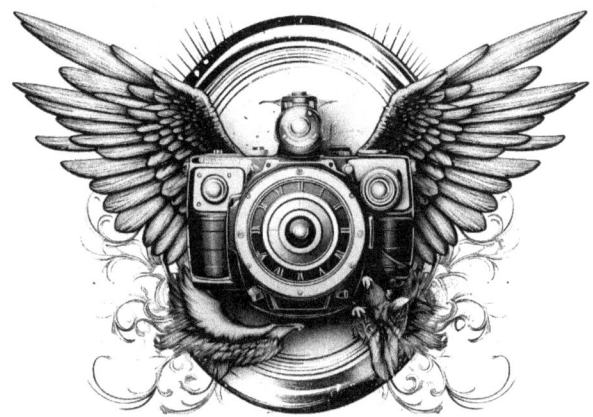

Camera lens with wings, representing a passion for photography and the freedom and perspective it brings to capture the world.

The Spirit Within

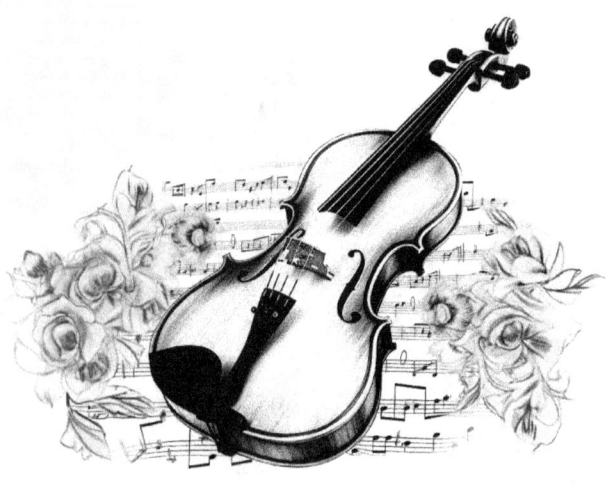

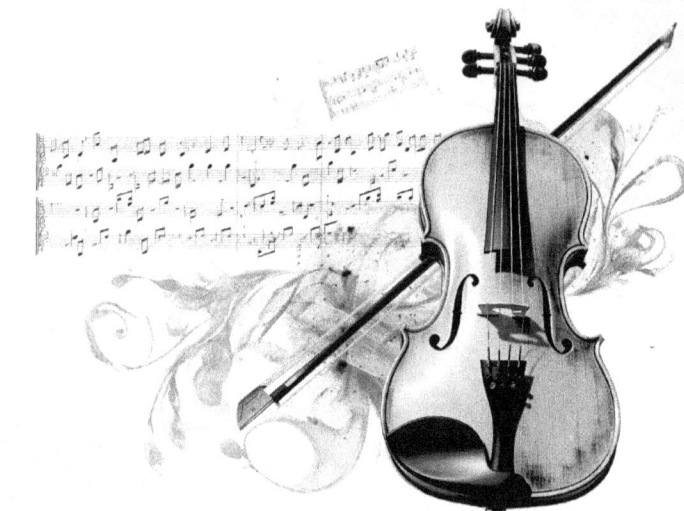

Detailed depiction of a violin and sheet music, representing a deep connection to the world of music and the pursuit of artistic passion.

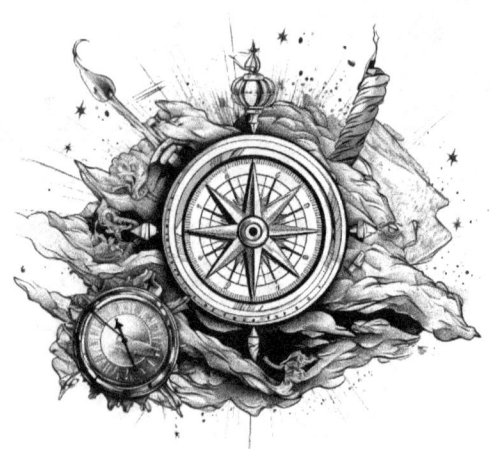

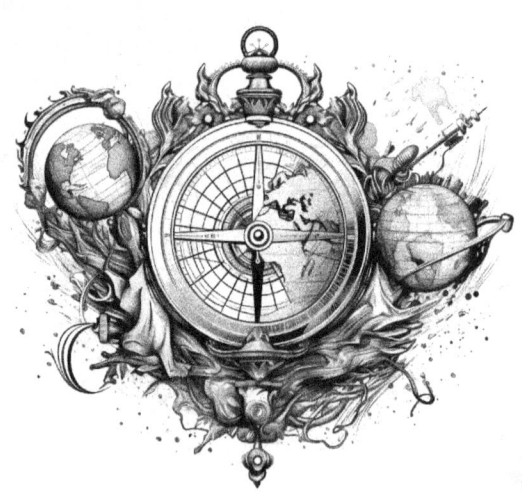

Detailed globe with a compass, symbolizing a passion for travel, exploration, and the quest for new experiences and perspectives.

The Spirit Within

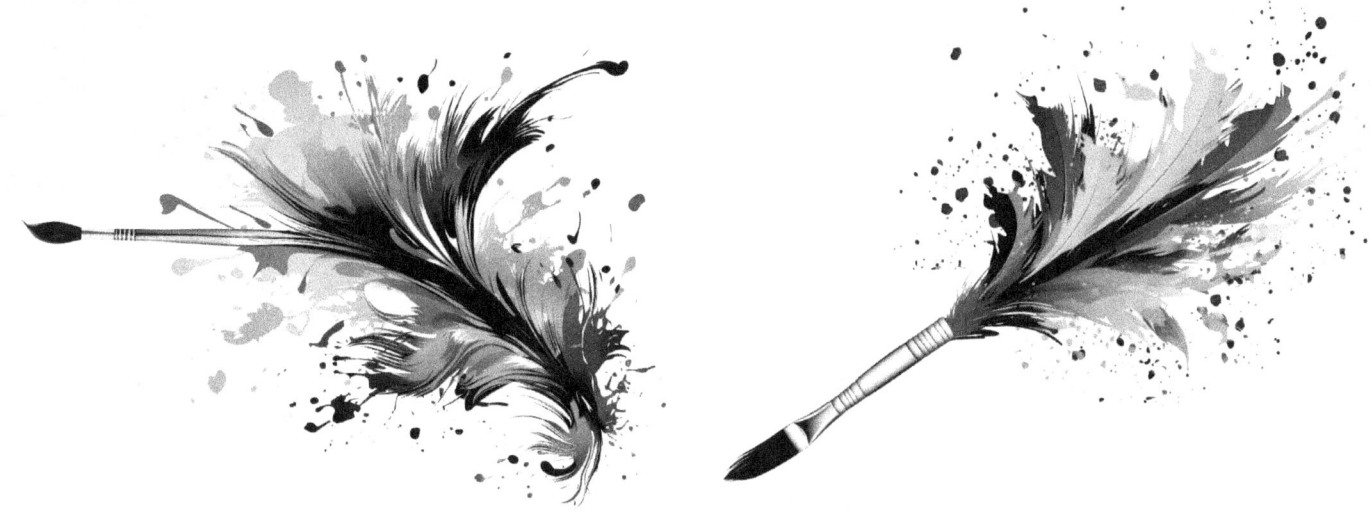

Paintbrush, symbolizing the joy,
freedom, and creative expression found
in the world of painting.

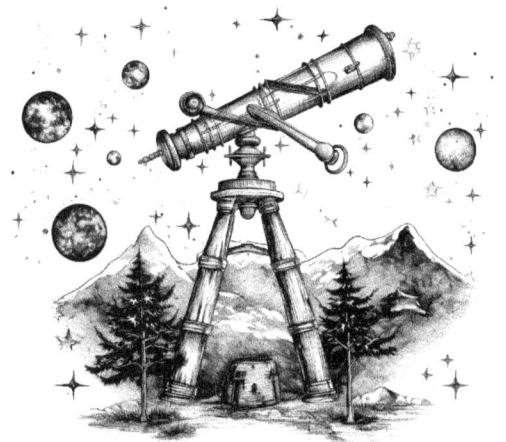
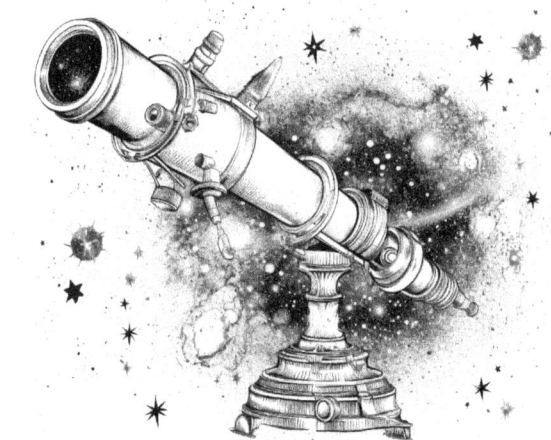

Telescope and constellations,
representing a passion for astronomy,
stargazing, and the wonders of the
universe.

The Spirit Within

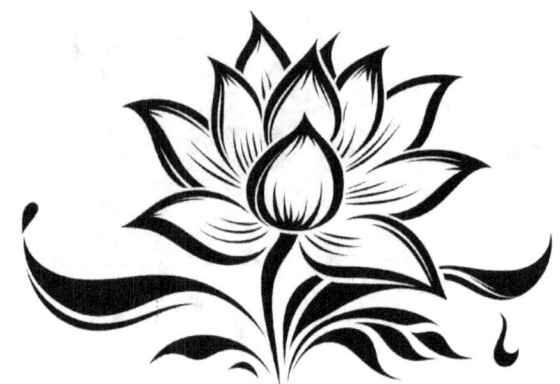

Lotus flower emerging from muddy waters, symbolizing the journey of personal growth, self-discovery, and finding one's purpose amidst life's challenges.

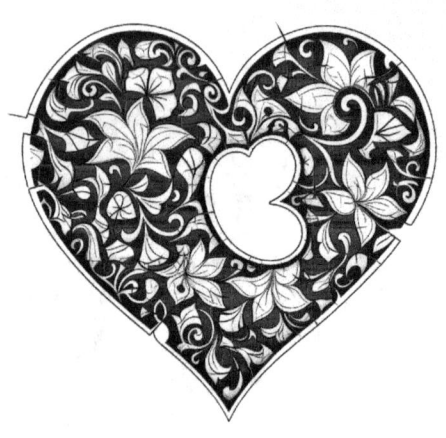

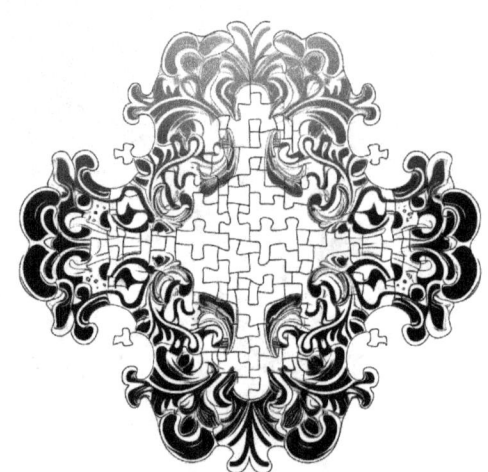

Jigsaw piece, symbolizing the importance of finding one's purpose, fitting into the bigger picture of life, and embracing one's unique gifts and talents.

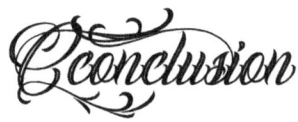

Conclusion

As we reach the pinnacle of this captivating journey through the realm of men's tattoo designs, a surge of awe and gratitude fills my being. "Tattoo Designs Book for Men" transcends the confines of a mere book; it is a testament to the boundless artistic prowess and the intricate narratives and symbolism concealed within extraordinary body art. It stands as a celebration of masculinity in its myriad forms, presenting an exquisite collection of designs that will ignite your imagination and leave an indelible imprint on your very soul.

As you reluctantly turn the pages, bidding farewell to "Tattoo Designs Book for Men," I hope a profound sense of inspiration, gratitude, and empowerment accompanies you on your journey. This book was meticulously crafted with unwavering passion and unwavering dedication, driven by an ardent appreciation for the artistry and storytelling woven into each tattoo. Your unwavering support and engagement have breathed life into these pages, infusing them with the energy of your own personal odyssey.

Embrace the boundless power emanating from within "Tattoo Designs Book for Men" and allow these designs to become an organic extension of your identity—an emblem of your resilience, strength, and steadfast commitment to self-expression. By adorning your skin with these extraordinary artistic expressions, you join a lineage of individuals who boldly challenge societal norms, reshaping the very definition of what it means to embody masculinity.

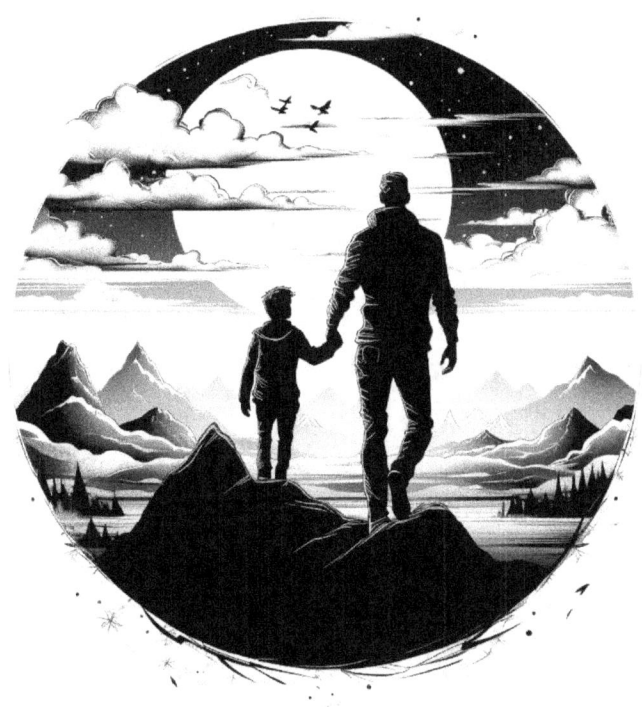

Thank You!!!

My sincerest gratitude accompanies you on this extraordinary adventure. Your investment in "Tattoo Designs Book for Men" extends far beyond a simple transaction; it symbolizes a profound connection to the essence of masculinity and a resolute dedication to unearthing the limitless depths of the human spirit. May your tattoos forever serve as a powerful testament to the transformative influence of inked artistry and the boundless potential that resides within your very being.

Lastly, if you have enjoyed your book we would greatly appreciate your support by leaving an honest review on Amazon. Thank you for being a valued member of our creative community!

Scan the QR Code:

Unlock a special bonus gift! As a thank you for your support, we are thrilled to offer you a free printable PDF of the entire book. Yes, you heard it right!

The complete collection of stunning tattoo designs illustrations is now available for you to enjoy in digital format, along with a <u>Bonus Surprise Gift</u>.

Experience the digital edition of "Tattoo Designs Book for Men" by emailing us at <u>opqaspace.press@gmail.com</u> with the subject line "TDBM". Delve into the captivating world of inked artistry from the convenience of your device. Claim your exclusive PDF copy and embark on a journey of self-expression. Request yours now and explore the remarkable designs at your own pace.